Deck on Deck

Towboating in the Twin Cities

By Capt. Bob Deck

Captain Bob Deck

Published by
Bob Deck
416 S. Lexington Pkwy.
St. Paul, MN 55105
www.deckondeck.com

With assistance from Riverwise, Inc.

Cover photo of Bob Deck by Brian Brezinka.
Back cover photo of Cullen Deck by his father, Bob Deck.

Dedicated to my grandfathers,
Vernon E. Deck and Robert I. Schjeldahl.

Grace Deck

Contents

Photographs

Introduction

Like Mark Twain, I signed on as a young lad to become a Mississippi riverboat pilot. Unlike him, I did not grow up along the banks of the Big Muddy dreaming of navigating this "strong brown god." Instead my childhood was spent on Air Force bases all over America, where I dreamed of piloting thundering jets, like my father.

However, the swirling currents of life carried me down a different channel to working the river. Before I could pilot I had to do my time on deck being trained by and working alongside of men every bit as colorful as Twain's characters. This book is about working the river with these unique people in a unique port during a historically significant time.

Right out of high school, in 1975, I began working aboard the towboats in the Port of St. Paul. At that time, towboat and barge traffic on the Upper Mississippi were in the middle of a tremendous boom. St. Paul and Minneapolis got swept along in those economic currents. The rapid growth attracted all sorts of characters to meet the demand for towboat crews. Some were easily identifiable from earlier river writers. Others reflected our unique times, including Vietnam veterans, hard-core bikers, artists and poets.

If you had a chance to watch the Mississippi River in the Twin Cities back in the 1970s, you would have seen dozens of steel-hulled towboats pushing barges. A dozen small harbor operators sprang up to compete with Twin City Barge & Towing. It was not uncommon to see four, five or even six towboats making round trips through the St. Anthony locks every day. The Port of Savage, on the Minnesota River, could easily load 40 barges a day to ship south to St. Louis and New Orleans. In St. Paul, more than a dozen docks bustled around the clock loading and unloading fertilizer, salt, cement, steel, coal and grain.

Times do change, and these twin ports are now barely recognizable to me. These days you would be lucky to see one or two boats pass downtown in a day, and there is only one towing company in town. Twin City

Barge's shipyard at Pigs Eye Lake was launching new barges every week back then, but now they mainly patch damaged barges. In South St. Paul, slips dredged to fleet hundreds of barges at a time have become islands covered with lush grasses, after the last two series of major floods.

These men and their stories are of a time gone by. Towboats and barges might one day disappear from the Twin Cities. The river in the Twin Cities is being gentrified and transformed into a more user-friendly tourist attraction. That may be for the best after all, but I will miss the wilder and more freewheeling river I grew up on.

Brian and Andy jerk up a wire and ratchet.

A Note from the First Mate

I met Captain Bob in a one-room schoolhouse when we were both seniors in high school. Bob left our high school humanities class six months early to continue his education at the River Academy. His goal was to become a riverboat pilot. All of us were fascinated with this exciting and novel career pursuit. We all stayed in touch at frequent gatherings where Bob was a popular guest in the off season. We enjoyed the way Bob spouted colorful maritime phrases and the escape his stories provided.

Over time we began dating, then married and had two great kids. I spent many boating seasons bringing the kids down to the wharf barge to pick up their dad and to see the towboats. They grew up going to barge pushes and pig roasts in the middle of the river. The kids knew to look for Bob when we drove over a bridge that crossed the river. When family and friends asked about his whereabouts, I often answered "he is at sea." During the winter layoffs Bob became the "parent on duty" and took great care of the kids while I worked.

Towboating in St. Paul is a shrinking industry, so Bob went back to school and earned his elementary teaching license. This opened a new chapter for Bob on the river. He has only become more passionate about boating on the Mississippi through curriculum development, teaching and cultivating a multidisciplinary network of river experts. Our son is grown and works part time on the river with him.

I know you'll enjoy my husband's stories. He makes the gritty existence of towboat pilots and deckhands irresistible. You will be able to hear his voice in the retelling of deckhand and towboat pilot experiences.

Be careful or your babies may grow up to be towboat captains.

Jean McMahon

Acknowledgements

My family deserves great thanks for their support, starting with my late mother, Ruth Louise Deck, and of course my wife, Jean McMahon, and our grown children, Cullen and Grace. They have all helped with the writing and some of the design of this book.

I owe thanks to some fellow river rats and sailors who have read my rough drafts and encouraged me to pursue publishing this book: John Halter, Jim Frisby, Brian Brezinka, Klaus Trieselmann, Doyle Deck, John Hatzung, Scott Bensen, Greg Oasheim, James "the Treeman" Carnahan, Big Red Coulthard and Jim McCoskey.

Several men with whom I worked have passed away too soon: Steamboat Bill Rupport, Col. Harry Baxter, Jeff Malm, Jimmy Hoffman and Bob Hayes.

And of course there is the Padelford gang, who have been supportive and helpful and have given me my latest home on the river: Capt. Gus Gaspardo, Tracy Shimek, Colleen "Bugg" O'Rourke, Gary Meyer, Shevek McKee, Cullen Deck, Matt Spence, Tommy Mega and the rest of the crew with four-, three-, two- and one-striped shirts.

Another person I owe thanks to is the gentleman who has spent time and effort editing this for me, Reggie McLeod.

Also, I would like to recognize the late Denise Anderson who was the fifth grade teacher for Cullen and Grace at Adam's Spanish Immersion. She helped me title this book before she passed away suddenly in June of 2009.

Glossary of Towboat Terms

chain strap — wire hoop with a three-foot length of heavy chain to anchor ratchets for tightening wires.

coaming — raised edge of the cargo hold of a barge. Deckhands walk between the edge of the barge and the coaming.

cow's-tail — length of twine cut from scrap pieces of line or rope.

fleet — a designated stretch along the bank where barges are secured by steel cables, shore wires anchored to the bank via steel pilings or large cement blocks.

H-bitt — main cleat on the bow of a tug. This large round pipe, six to 12 inches in diameter, is welded into an "H" shape and used to secure strong deck lines to pull on grounded barges.

kevel — anvil-shaped peg on the deck of a barge for securing a wire.

light boat — to drive without barges in front of the boat.

line boat — the customer of harbor boats. They are the big boats pushing as many as 15 barges between St. Paul and St. Louis.

load — loaded barge. Empties weigh about 250 tons, and loads weigh nearly 1,300 tons.

ratchet — large turnbuckle with a pelican hook on each end for securing the end of a wire to chain links on the deck. They are tightened to pull the barges tightly together.

ship-ups — the clutch-throttle combos on the console in the pilothouse that modern diesel pilots use to control the engine in forward and reverse.

tie-off cell — large, round, steel-walled structure about 12 feet in diameter filled with sand or cement. Kevels or timberheads are fixed to the top to hold ropes or lines.

timberhead — classic bollard used to secure heavy marine vessels. Usually a twelve-inch-thick, walled, steel cylinder about two feet high. The best ones are narrower at the base and flared at the top.

toothpick — one- or two-foot long, half-inch to an inch-thick steel rod (rebar or old axles) to slip through the pelican hook and prevent a ratchet (large turnbuckle) from spinning freely while being tightened.

towknee — the large triangular-shaped steel structure on the bow of a towboat that makes contact with the barges. Towboats have two towknees, one on each side of the bow.

wire — 35-foot length of steel cable used to tie barges together. A loop at one end fits over a kevel and the opposite end has a smaller nickel-swedged eye that fits the pelican hook of a ratchet.

Getting Buzzed on the Upper Mississippi

M ark Twain wrote that his greatest ambition was to become a river pilot, and many of the men who work on the river today grew up along the banks and watched the massive rafts of barges being guided by mighty diesel-powered towboats. But the Mississippi River never aroused any curiosity in me as a child. I never read about it or wondered about it or any of the lifestyles that were part of the lore of the Mississippi. My only dream as a young boy was to be a jet-fighter pilot like my father.

My childhood was spent on Air Force bases all over the country, except for three years my family lived on the small Pacific island of Okinawa at Kadena Air Force Base. I built model airplanes and flew them all over the house and dreamed of being a fighter pilot like my dad. Dad even started giving me flying lessons in a small Cessna, when I was in sixth grade. So it was very weird when I found myself one morning in the spring of 1975 on the Upper Mississippi River standing on the steel deck of a barge loaded with 1,300 tons of coal.

The barge was grouped with a bunch of others in a slough across from Prescott, Wisconsin. It was early morning and the misty fog from the surrounding woods poured gently into the slough. It crept around the trunks of the cottonwoods and swirled out over the water. The branches of the cottonwoods were full of early-spring buds.

On the far side of the slough a great blue heron, knee deep in the shoreline mud, carefully high stepped over and then ducked under the weathered limbs of a dead tree lying on its side. He took a half hearted stab at a fish and then slowly unfolded his wings. With a slight bob he pushed down with his wings spread and was airborne. Gliding through the mist just inches from the surface of the river he was the undisputed king of this primordial scene.

His flight path carried him up over the fog and across the width of the slough. He glided on across the primeval scene until he spied the gleaming white and blue steel diesel towboat, the motor vessel *Sioux*.

The first thing to notice about towboats is that they are rectangular. There are few of the graceful lines found on other kinds of boats. The hull is a long squat rectangle and each deck above is a smaller rectangle topped off by the pilothouse arrayed with searchlights, antennae and radar sweeps. The bow end has huge triangles welded on it to push the barges. It takes years of being around these ungainly looking craft to appreciate them for what they can do.

The heron must not have seen one before, because he let out a long, low, angry croak. The towboat and long barges full of saw-toothed piles of greasy coal and all the associated noise was upsetting him.

He looked down at the barge where the other two deckhands and I were standing. He let out another irritated squawk and voided his bowels on the deck in front of us. Then with a tip of his wings he turned to glide once more past the towboat *Sioux* pushing the barges. A thicker wall of fog gobbled him up, as he glided away from the modern contraptions.

The *Sioux* was commanded by a grizzled old captain nicknamed Paleface, for his ability to turn ghost white in a crisis. The other crew members consisted of one engineer, a cook and three deckhands who were occupied with rigging a raft of nine loaded coal barges to tow up the St. Croix River to the Allen S. King power plant. The barges had been delivered overnight by a boat from the St. Paul harbor. The coal was loaded into barges from Montana railcars in Minneapolis, not far from Broadway Avenue and I-94.

By far the youngest member of the crew, at 17, I had signed onto the *Sioux* as an inexperienced "green" deckhand. I watched as the heron swooped on past us and disappeared into the low-lying fog again.

"Can you believe that silly bird trying to crap all over our beautiful morning kid?" Old Charlie said with an earsplitting grin.

Larry retorted "I'd as soon shoot that damn bird is what I'd like to do."

The *Sioux* was faced up on one of the loads and pushing it across the slip to another barge. I was setting up a couple sets of rigging for the first coupling. The experienced deckhands teaching me the ropes — a couple of real old timers named Charlie and Larry — were bickering as usual.

"What are you doing letting the kid lay the wires?" Larry sneered. He leaned against the bulkhead of the barge with one hand nursing a cigarette and the other buried inside his baggy bib overalls.

Larry was big, portly and had thinning reddish hair. He wore wire-rimmed glasses and blue and white pin-striped bib overalls. He was always leaning on something, scratching and smoking. His acidic temperament came from the terrible burden of being better and smarter than everyone around him.

"He needs to learn how to run the stuff out and set up the wires for three-ways," muttered Charlie.

Old Charlie was somewhere between 60 and older than steamboats. Unlike Larry he still loved working the river and wasn't yet fed up with people. He was ancient looking but young at heart and far happier with his lot in life. Decking was perfect for him, and he was laid back on the subject. It allowed him to drink every evening in the waterfront bars of Prescott and have a safe warm bed to crash into each night at closing time.

Larry snapped back, "Well if he screws 'em up, you get to straighten them out."

I ran out a ratchet pretending not to hear.

A ratchet is a long turnbuckle device for pulling rigging wires tight. It has a hollow "barrel" about the length and thickness of a baseball bat. Each hollow end has a three-foot-long arm that screws in and out of it. The end of each arm had a "pelican hook" that closes over and holds onto one end of the wire or a set of chain links that acts as an anchor against which to pull the wire tight. The chain links are anchored to a fitting on one of the barges.

When two or more barges are setting together in the proper arrangement the wire is wrapped around fittings between two barges. One of the pelican hooks is clamped to hold the loose "small eye" of the wire. Two deckhands take hold of the ratchet and "jerk it up" as tight as they are able. The free pelican hook on the opposite end is then fastened into one of the chain links. One of the deckhands then tightens the ratchet by using the long handle welded onto the middle of the barrel. When the wire gets tight the deckhand slips a five foot long pipe over the handle to use as a "cheater bar" and get the inch thick cables tighter than a fiddle string. Sixty or 70 such "sets" of rigging can hold a dozen to 15 barges tight enough to steer all the way to St. Louis.

By the time I had the ratchet almost run out to its fullest length, Larry had both hands overhead holding them closer and closer together until at last his palms clapped together.

"You're up Captain." He mumbled to himself.

Gently the barge we were standing on touched up against another barge. At the same moment half of the ratchet I was preparing to use fell apart and clanged to the deck at my feet. I looked stupidly at the other two and waited for Larry's words of encouragement.

"Wonderful he ran it out too far. We're supposed to build this tow and the dumb bastard is breaking the tools!"

"Aww shuddup! It ain't but a second to fix. Rethread it Junior. That's right, line the arm up with the barrel and wind the turnbuckle back in."

"Toldja the kid was too stupid to do anything by hisself."

There was a crackle in the air as the loudspeaker on top of the *Sioux* pilothouse was powered up. "You all boys got that couplin' tight yet?"

Larry looked back 200 feet to the boat and swung his right arm back and forth horizontally at shoulder height. "No, not yet. Junior here, your college-boy, screwed it up."

"Thanks Larry," I said under my breath as I set about to screw the two ends of my ratchet back together.

Charlie and Larry laid the wires down and snatched them up tight. I bent over and started putting toothpicks into the pelican hooks of one of the ratchets. Larry suddenly clammed up and shushed Charlie and me. "Quiet! What's that sound?"

When I straightened up to wipe my forehead with the back of my glove, the two old coots stopped jawing for a minute. From somewhere beyond the tree line there was a faint but growing sound. It wasn't like any of the other wildlife around here. Three sets of ears perked up and three faces lifted at the same time to see a small plane hop over the tree line and dive straight at us. It happened so fast and unexpectedly that none of us could move.

The plane continued to aim straight at us and leveled off only 10 feet above the piles of coal. It blew by right over our heads close enough that we could make out the rivets along the fuselage and the slight streak of oil running aft from the engine cowling. The noise was deafening at that range.

We turned together and watched as it headed straight for the pilothouse of the *Sioux*. Even 200 feet from the boat we could clearly see the stunned look on the captain's face. He had the coffee pot in one hand and a cup in the other, while his face contorted from disbelief to sheer terror. When he saw the plane about to crash into the boat's pilothouse, he dropped the coffee pot and cup and flew out the side door of the pilothouse.

In a cartoon flash he was climbing over the handrail to abandon ship. Paleface had one leg over and was just about to roll across the handrail and drop 40 feet to the river, when the plane powered up and over the pilothouse of the *Sioux*.

I looked at the faces of Larry and Charlie. Their open-mouthed stares must have been the same look that primitive South Sea islanders had when they saw Amelia Earhart fly overhead.

I looked back to the captain still half over the handrail. Slowly he regained his composure and straightened up to watch the small plane disappear over the trees. Out on the barges the two older men looked at each other blinking like deer in a headlight.

The loudspeaker on top of the pilothouse crackled loudly, "Holy smoking sunnovabich! Didja see that crazy fool? Didja?" Paleface was back inside now wiping his face and scanning the tree line for the phantom plane.

Now composed again and acting as if it had never happened, Larry turned to us and muttered "Naw, we never saw a thing you dumb SOB!" Then turning back to the boat he held both hands over his head and clasped them together. "Tow's ready to go Cappy!" he yelled loud enough for the people of Prescott to hear across the river.

Paleface yelled back, "Good! Turn these barges loose, and let's get outta here! I wanna forget this morning ever happened!"

Old Charlie was still scratching his whiskers, "Well now that is somethin' you don't see every day now isn't it?" Larry just gave him a disgusted look.

Before we could turn the tow loose from the bank, the *Sioux* needed to be "knocked out" from the barge on the outside corner of the tow and reset in the middle of the three strings to balance the steering and handling of the tow.

A towboat is held tightly to a barge with a strong cable on each side of the boat. They are as thick as a wrist and run from the middle of the boat out to the barge and then back to a heavy-duty winch on the bow of the boat. Usually two men handle a wire together. It can be done by one strong guy with the proper technique and body mechanics. I wasn't in possession of that knowledge or skill just yet.

"Don't lift that by yourself," Larry hissed. "You'll get hurt."

Leaning back with all my 145 pounds, I jerked upwards until the wire was clear of the deck fitting. When I stood to walk it sideways over to the towknee of the boat, it damn near pulled me off the barge. The 10 feet I had to move over was a Herculean struggle for me at that slight weight. In the middle of the activity I felt a hot burning sensation in my neck and shoulders, but I wasn't about to let on to Larry that I hurt myself. He was smirking.

"Okay kid, if it's so easy get the other one by yourself."

I swallowed hard and took a deep breath, but Charlie hurried over to help me. "Don't do anything that bum tells ya to do kid. Stick by me and listen to me. He'll just get you in trouble."

"Thanks Charlie."

Once the boat was faced up to the center barge, we walked out to the bow end of the tow double-checking all the couplings and wires to make sure that all were tight and the loads were secure.

On the far end from the boat, out on the bow of the tow, we stopped for a moment. Larry said "Finish tightenin' that wire on the head Junior, and we'll turn the high captain loose!"

Larry and old Charlie headed down the outside of the barges to unwrap the steel shore wires from the tow, and I bent back down to crank away on the ratchet handle. The wire between the two barges got tighter, and I was alone with my thoughts. There was something about that small plane that stuck in my head.

Up in the pilothouse Paleface was busy cleaning up his mess and nervously ducking imaginary dive bombers. I was only alone for a few minutes when Charlie and Larry scurried back around the corner to where I was still cranking away on a ratchet. One of them spoke, "Hey Junior stop a minute wouldja?"

Then we heard the sound again. This time he came out of the sun. The plane was in a steep dive this time, headed right for us on the barges. Larry and Charlie dropped to the deck, but I just stood there. The plane pulled up and up until it was aimed again at the pilothouse. "Oh noooo! Not again!" came over the loudspeaker. Again the, now only half-full, coffee pot went up into the air, and Paleface was out the door with one leg over the rail. His face was even more terrified than the first time.

Again the plane snapped straight up, and this time I could see a red sunburst splashed across the shiny white paint on the topside of the wing. The sound of the engine grew more powerful as the plane finished off a high loop over the barges.

My stomach tightened, not from fear but because I was familiar with the feeling you get when a plane like that goes inverted. There was also something very familiar about that particular airplane.

In a moment the plane leveled off, banked sharply and flew off towards St. Paul, while the pilot waggled his wings. Larry was chuckling, now back on his feet, "Hey look at the high captain — he's so scared he don't know whether to shit or wind his watch."

While he waited for us to finish the tow building, Captain Paleface bobbed and weaved up there between the steering sticks, watching out for kamikazes and ghosts. "What are you all waitin' for? Turn the tow loose, and let's get the hell away from here!"

Larry was shaking his head as he and Charlie scanned the horizon for another attack. "What in the hell was that?" Charlie kept muttering.

"Some kinda crazy dive-bomber," said Larry.

"Oh that was a Citabria," I interrupted. "It's a stunt flier, not a dive-bomber."

They turned to me and gave me a look as if I had just stepped out of a flying saucer. "Well Junior," Larry sneered, "just how in the hell do you know that?"

Before I could think I blurted out "Well because that was my dad flyin' it!"

Immediately I knew that my riposte had not been well played.

Larry simply blinked and looked from my face back towards the boat. The captain was busy in the pilothouse wiping coffee up off the floor and the console. The console has all of the pilot's controls — rudder levers, air control throttles for the main engines, an assortment of switches for navigation lights and searchlights — that can get gummed up with spilled liquids. Paleface wiped furiously to get the stuff off of his workstation.

Larry took a step towards me "Well, whatever ya do don't let the captain find out you're related to that crazy bastard, or he'll ride your ass for the rest of the summer. Probably take it out on the whole crew too."

The pilot of that plane was my father, a retired USAF combat-proven fighter pilot by the name of Major Eddie V. Deck. After 150 missions over North Vietnam in a Republic F-105 "Thud," the act of buzzing a sitting towboat was just "plane" fun. When he was flying missions over North Vietnam the route they took followed the mountains bordering the Red River. The Thud pilots called themselves river rats.

For a brief moment I felt superior to that crabby old bastard Larry. Only a few years before I had sat poolside at Nellis Air Force Base when the Thunderbirds would practice. A formation of Phantom aircraft thundering right overhead was more familiar to me than all the nature that surrounded me now. Here was something intruding in his element that I was comfortable with, and it had him stumped.

My dad was a guy born to fly. His father named him Eddie Vernon after the first combat flying ace the United States ever produced. Growing up in Los Angeles, he watched the skies constantly for a sight of an airplane. In grade school he saved bottle caps for a contest and won a 15-minute ride over LA in a C-47. From there he joined the Air Force and became one of the most talented pilots this country has ever trained.

After dad retired from the Air Force he took a job flying for Twin City Barge & Towing Company. The river barge business was going through a boom time, and they needed their president to fly back and forth to Washington to lobby for the industry. The company liked the idea of entrusting their president to a proven pilot.

One day during the fall of my last year in high school he came to me, "Hey do you want to work on the river?"

"Well I don't know. What's it like?" We only moved to Minnesota when he retired. All I had ever known were Air Force Bases from one end of the country to the other. Since moving here I'd never even been down to the river. The only times I had bothered to even look at it was from the bridge between St. Paul and Fort Snelling on my way out to my high school job at the old Met Stadium.

"You'll figure it out. You might as well take it, since I'm not sending you to college."

"I guess I'm going to learn about working on the river."

So while my high school classmates rented tuxedos and bought prom dresses, I got fitted for steel-toed boots and leather work gloves. Growing up as an Air Force brat meant I had seen a good bit of the world, but this was my first time on the Mississippi River. It was a body of water I had only heard of in school but which was about to become my whole world.

By the time we got back to the boat Captain Paleface had the tow backing out of the slough and into the main channel of the Mississippi. We clambered over the splashboard onto the head-deck and stopped dead in our tracks. A large rat, nearly the size of a housecat, scurried out of the forward deck locker and onto the deck at our feet. It took one long look at us and scampered to the starboard side of the boat. He hopped up onto one of the fittings along the edge of the deck, where he turned and took one last look at us before he dove into the river.

"Huh! Ya don't see that every day. Wonder if'n he wasn't trying to tell us something," joked Charlie.

Larry took a long drag on his cigarette and answered slowly, "Well whaddaya think he was tryin' to say?" Then he scowled at me, "I think the wrong rat jumped boat on us."

The replay of the incident came up at the galley table over supper. Paleface was still a bit shaken. Larry glowered at me for a brief moment.

"I got half a mind to call the FAA and report that crazy sumbitch," Paleface muttered.

Larry jumped at the chance, "Kid here knows who the pilot is Cappy."

"Is that so?" Paleface looked at me.

I was too scared to speak, so Larry continued, "Yeah it was his old man. The guy who flies for the company." He forced a sly smile my way.

Paleface looked at me again and then he slowly said, "Oh hell, the damn Feds would think I was just another dumb towboat pilot seen a UFO or a flying saucer or something."

He looked thoughtful for a minute and then said to me, "Say kid — ya don't suppose next time he wants to say 'hi' he could just drive over or phone ya?"

But the sight of him flying low over the tree line waggling his wings was one of the last times I saw him. He flew out of my life not long after that. I learned that he did a little crop-dusting in the Mississippi Delta cotton fields and even delivered corporate jets all over the globe for Cessna before he passed away in 2001.

But he passed me onto the river rats who finished raising me during one of the most interesting periods on the Mississippi. It was a boom time on the river. The boom created many jobs and attracted a wide variety of new-age river rats. The adventure of working on the barges and the art of piloting was as challenging as when steam was king. The men who worked on the river in those times grew up hearing about the life from their river rat fathers or they found their way there after duty in Vietnam — duty that left many of them unable to adjust to nine-to-five jobs and perfect for the roustabout life on a Mississippi River boat.

Most people who live in the Twin Cities of St. Paul and Minneapolis take little notice of the Mississippi River at their feet. Even when they pass over any of the dozens of bridges that link the bluffs on either side of the river, they barely bother to look at it.

I learned that the Mississippi River is as romantic today as when steamboats ran over sandbars and navigated rocky rapids. Powerful diesel tow-boats pushing acres of steel barges down a river manacled by locks and dams does not diminish the charm and character of Old Man River.

Steamboat Bill and his Merry Band — Steel Toes and White Mules

My first month on the Mississippi had been spent living the good life aboard the *Sioux* with my private room, warm bunk, three huge home-cooked meals a day and time to lounge around talking to the old timers and reading novels. But after a pleasant month-long introduction to river life aboard the *Sioux*, the folks at Twin City Barge decided I needed to see the St. Paul harbor, and start learning how deckhands work in the harbor. I was assigned to a towboat called the *Pawnee* working the fleets of South St. Paul. These fleets are the staging area for all the operations that feed the terminals in Minneapolis and in Savage, up the Minnesota River.

They sent me to catch the *Pawnee* at the wharf barge in Pigs Eye Lake. On the way to the WB I drove through an industrial corridor of grain-loading docks, steel plants, a cement plant and an oil refinery.

So when I walked over the levee to the ramp leading down to the WB, I was surprised at the wilderness of Pigs Eye Lake. Beyond the wharf and the surrounding barge fleet was Pigs Eye Island, which separated the slip from the main channel of the Mississippi. Later I learned that the island was the biggest heron rookery along the Upper Mississippi and home to thousands of snowy egrets. Upstream, beyond all this, rose the brief skyline of St. Paul.

East of the skyline Dayton's Bluff loomed over Pigs Eye Lake itself and a cattail swamp teeming with waterfowl. The slough behind the island had been dredged into a long slip that links Pigs Eye Lake to the main channel of the Mississippi River.

When I turned around and looked downstream, I could see the main channel of the Mississippi down to the I-494 Bridge. A big line boat had just put the coals to a raft of barges. Smoke poured from the twin stacks as the whole thing slid around the bend above the bridge.

The WB is the nerve center of a harbor operation. It is where the boats lay-up, fuel up, crew up and get repaired after a screw-up. Across the slip was a loose fleet of empty barges waiting to be cleaned or repaired before being reloaded.

A young man with sandy blonde hair and a beard was walking past the ramp when he stopped to look me over. I was dressed in my River Academy khaki pants and shirt with my brand-new steel-toed boots. On my hands were my brand new pair of White Mule work gloves. The leather was dyed a light blue, and they were spotless. He took one more look at me and snorted in disbelief, "Who are you? Are you my new deckhand? You're my new deckhand!? What in the hell am I supposed to do with a pipsqueak like you?"

I managed to stammer, "Well they told me to catch a harbor tug called the *Pawnee*."

"Well my name's Bill, but these clowns down here call me Steamboat," he looked down at my feet again. "Don't wear out that fancy pair of boots kid!"

I was dumbfounded. "What do you mean?" I looked down at my work boots to see what could be wrong.

"Don't wear out that first pair of work boots. That's what the old timers say, because if you wear out that first pair of boots, if you stay on the river long enough to wear a pair of boots out, you'll be hooked. The river will have you, she'll be in your blood, and she'll never let you go." He paused again and looked at me. "What's your name?"

"Robert Deck." I answered. He chuckled

"Okay Bobby Deck the deckhand, come on down to the boat. I want you to meet Tommy Towboater and Bill Barge. They're deckhands too."

Then he rolled his eyes and turned to walk towards one of the boats tied alongside the wharf barge we were standing on.

"So tell me Junior, what kind of experience do you have?"

"Well — I took the two month safety course at the River School, and I spent the last month working on the *Sioux*."

He harrumphed. "You mean riding right? They don't do any real work on deck. Do they?"

I stammered back "Well Larry and Charlie taught me to lay fore and aft wires."

"You better know how to lay fore and aft wires. That's the least of what we do. When I'm done with ya, you'll know how to whip 15 loads together — or I'll throw your ass in the river!"

I was afraid to move, a little intimidated by this crusty old river rat, 24 years of age. But then his blue eyes twinkled over his thick sandy beard, and he broke into a wide grin. "C'mon I'll show you to our fine vessel." He turned to walk towards the other end of the wharf, and I fell into his wake while trying to take it all in.

Steamboat Bill was the "fleet mate" of the St. Paul harbor. He was responsible for rigging all the barges heading southbound for St. Louis out of the Twin Cities. He was the high priest of rigging barges, as I would soon learn.

The deck of the 200-foot-long wharf was topped with asphalt. The entire thing was covered in a high ceiling corrugated steel shed. Around the perimeter of the shed about every ten feet was a timberhead or a large cleat for the harbor tugs to tie off on. Inside was a ship's store that had anything a deckhand could need: gloves, steel-toed boots, serrated knives, rain gear, flashlights and other marine odds-n-ends. One end of the wharf was a machine shop, where the mechanics repaired diesel engines, generators and even the heavy-duty hydraulic deck winches used for sucking towboats up tight to barges. The smell was an overwhelming mixture of rust and diesel.

Lying around everywhere were spools and lengths of scrap pieces of wire as thick as a big man's wrist. The barge business lives by wires. Wires hold the barges together, hold the boat to the tow of barges and moor the barges along the banks from here to New Orleans.

At the other end of the wharf was my new assignment, the mighty motor vessel *Pawnee*. Compared to the large, well kept and shiny *Sioux,* this thing was a beater. It listed 10 degrees to one side and was covered in grease. How could this thing be operational? Surely it must be in some stage of repair or salvage.

"Here she is, the mighty vessel *Pawnee*. I know she ain't much to look at, but you'll get used to her." He saw the look of disgust on my face. "Yeah she's no *Sioux* to be sure, but remember, this is no riding line boat, this is a harbor boat and St. Paul is the busiest harbor on the Upper Miss."

Steamboat Bill stepped over the splashboard onto a head deck covered with ratchets, wires and several stacks of coiled and well used synthetic ropes. He motioned for me to follow him with a disdainful look. "Don't ever let anyone hear you call these ropes. Ropes is for cows. We tie barges off with lines."

Then he turned and stuck his finger in my face, "And rule number one is: Don't fall in! If you fall in the river, you are dead! It's that simple."

"Well, yeah. I guess I wouldn't want to drown."

"Hah! You'd be lucky to drown! More'n likely you'd get chopped into pieces by the propellers. They'd suck you right under the boat and cut you into bait."

Baptism

Four pair of strong hands held me down on the deck of the *Pawnee* as she was sinking bow first into the brown swirling water of the Mississippi River. I was trapped, and the water was rising fast around me. No matter how hard I struggled, I couldn't escape the water creeping up my boots and my legs.

My back was jammed in between the posts of the H-bitts welded to the head deck. All I could see was blue sky above and big, fat, puffy clouds. The river continued to rise up my back, and the rotten smell of the South St. Paul stockyards crept into my nose. "Aghh!" I groaned and squirmed against the men holding me down.

My frustration was starting to turn to cold panic when I heard the double "whoosh, whoosh" as the pilot pulled both main engines out of gear, stopping the huge propellers from pushing the boat forward.

The boat labored like a stunned boxer to rise back out of the river. Water poured back down off of my back and my legs. My boots were still full of water and maybe what felt like a couple of minnows wriggling around. The hands that held me down released me. I rolled over and slumped to the deck. I struggled to catch my breath. The water continued to pour down the slope of the deck and off the sides of the boat into the river. A lot of the water had pooled up at the base of the forward bulkhead between the deck winches. I spied a couple of synthetic ropes floating around in this little pool.

I knelt there still catching my breath. I was grandly pissed as I looked up into the faces of the grinning deck-apes surrounding me.

"Hey you look real green now Greenie! Har, har!"

"You gone down on the *Pawnee* now Kid!" said a second voice.

"This is your official river baptism boy!" said a third.

Then Steamboat added, "Kid you gotta learn when to keep your mouth shut."

Steamboat Bill demonstrates the proper way to handle a face wire.

I just sat there on the cold wet steel deck as they, one-by-one, slapped me on the back and headed back down the port side of the boat and disappeared into the bunk room. They were overjoyed to be getting a huge break from our regular grind and a ride all the way up to a barge fleet underneath the Robert Street Bridge in downtown St. Paul.

This was my hazing into the crew of the harbor towboat *Pawnee*. It was a ritual they men referred to as "going down on the *Pawnee*." It was performed in response to some numbskull smart-assed remark I made. I don't even remember what I said, but it probably added to the reputation I needed to shake as a college boy from the River Academy.

On wobbly legs, I stood and looked up at the pilothouse. The square steel box with slanted roof was all the way down on the hydraulic ram. Captain Murphy leaned out the open pilothouse window to grin at me. His silver-gray hair was pomaded into a sort of wave from the part on one side, in the style of southern pilots. "Well kid ya gotta go along to get along," was all he said. And then he was gone, but a second later I could see his feet up on the console. So I was the only one not relaxing on our one long break of a trip from tow work.

Each time Murphy moved the steering levers, the long skinny *Pawnee* rolled like a drunken sailor. Without a barge to harness the power of the barn-door-sized towboat rudders, she wanted to just roll over. I steadied myself between the safety chains strung from the edge of the deck to the overhang of the second deck and the handrail welded along the length of the bulkheads.

Halfway down the side of the vessel I paused and peered into the engine room door. The air smelled saturated with diesel fumes and exhaust. The twin caterpillar engines had exhaust pipes leading up through the second deck ceiling. But enough exhaust leaked from the various joints to leave the white painted walls stained light gray to black.

Standing in the din of diesel engines, turbochargers, the many hydraulic pumps and motors was like being inside a jet engine, so I moved back to the bunkroom door.

This room was only slightly cleaner than the engine room. Sets of bunk beds were fixed along two of the walls. On each of the bunks was a ratty mattress coated with grime that made my skin crawl. On each mattress one of the crew stretched out like he was in a five-star hotel.

Steamboat Bill and his merry band were all guys in their mid-twenties from International Falls, Minnesota: "Pig Man," "Whispering Kevin" and "Sparks." They were a smorgasbord of northern Minnesota Viking types. I had a ways to go to fit in with these roughnecks. They had already figured me out. I was this goofy kid who showed up for deck work one day in a khaki cadet uniform. It was the first time I heard a phrase I would hear a lot the next couple of years: "So you're going to be a pilot. Huh. Well it takes more than a buncha books to make a pilot. Hell, ya cain't make a pilot outta no damn books!"

I went back to the galley to eat my sandwich.

Life on the *Sioux* had been grand compared to this. I had my own room with fresh sheets on the bed, hot meals served three times a day and just enough tow work in the morning to make for a nice workout each day. Otherwise, I observed the beauty of the St. Croix River and read science fiction novels, while we pushed coal barges back and forth from the King power plant near Stillwater.

Behind the old electric stove in the galley was a large round scorch mark where some deckhand had set his lunch on fire. From inside the mold-ridden refrigerator I gently lifted my peanut butter sandwich from the one relatively clean spot on a shelf. I scooched into the booth-style table seat and sat with my elbows resting on the yellowed linoleum countertop.

When I was done eating, I walked over to put the empty plastic bag in the large chrome garbage can. The boat rolled unexpectedly and my thigh bumped the can hard enough to tip it over. Underneath was a huge colony of maggots. After a gulp of fresh air at the door, I set about sweeping them up and turned to throw them overboard along with the dustpan I never wanted to see again.

"What did I do to deserve this?" I thought. I was feeling pretty sorry for myself. Only a few days after Steamboat Bill had welcomed me aboard, I was convinced I wouldn't last another week on the river.

Tow Building and Fleet Work
on a Lunch-bucket Boat

The crew of the *Pawnee* had three main duties: assist northbound line boats into the fleets of St. Paul, "strip" or remove the wire rigging from the just arrived barges and rerig the barges after they were loaded for the trip back southbound.

Our part of the world, our little stretch of the river, was limited to the few miles between St. Paul and Newport. The only time we got near St. Paul was to work in American Commercial Barge Line's fleet up around the Holman Field Airport. From ACBL fleet we could glimpse the tall buildings of downtown and get a sense of life with real people.

Since I was on the *Pawnee* to learn tow building, my view was focused mostly on Bill, barge fittings, cleats, kevels, timberheads, ratchets, wires, chain slings and lines.

Wiring up a southbound tow solid enough for a trip to St. Louis requires a lot of skill. The rigging is cumbersome, the fittings on the barges are not uniform, and the mates on several line boats have weird requirements that need be attended to. Possibly the hardest part was getting all the leads right and making them work. A lead is the direction a wire runs to hold strings of barges from sliding back and forth while the big boats steer. A corner where four barges meet has four wires all going in opposite directions that looks like an "11" with a capital "X" superimposed on top of it. It's sort of like a greasy cat's cradle.

Steamboat Bill took his fleet-mate position seriously and took great pride in his tow-building skills. He could lay that rigging fast and clean. It is important that the wires slide around one another. This is so they are easy to jerk up and can be tightened without binding. Even experienced mates sometimes lay rigging that has to be beaten on to tighten, and that makes one pretty tired after 12 hours.

Spend a day building tows. Crank on the ratchet. Pull the four-foot cheater bar off of the ratchet handle. Walk over and slam it down hard on the one lead of your wire to pop it loose. Feel your hands get numb. Step over and tighten some more. Twelve hours of this leaves even strong men exhausted. But with Bill's style of rigging, we rarely had to fight with the rigging.

Days and weeks of tow building start to run together in a blur, but Bill never seemed to tire. He was a tow-building machine, a genius. His attitude was like a scientist or an artist. He approached a tow like a sculptor looks at a fresh hunk of granite.

He'd get down on his knees and peer through the centers of kevels, between timberheads, look at the other leads for room to travel his wires. When satisfied he had found an avenue, he'd thread those heavy stiff wires as easy as a seamstress. Those wires that he spent a few extra seconds to properly lay tightened faster and easier, ultimately saving time and energy.

Wires laid improperly get old and kinky. These are the wires that bite and slap and kick like an abused dog or a kid. After you force one of the kinks around a fitting, it will snap back and crack you in the shin or forehead if you are bent over.

Every green deckhand has a time when the mate is wrestling with just such a wire and has both hands full and probably a foot or two as well. He might look like Tarzan fighting off a 20-foot boa constrictor made of steel. The poor green man is at a loss. He wants to help but has no idea where to jump into this man-sized mouse trap of a cat's cradle.

Bill yells at me to "fight, fart or hold the light, but for Christ's sake do something!"

Later when the rigging is just about all laid up, and all there is to do is tighten, Bill walks back and forth across the barges. He stops by the wires each of us is tightening and jumps up and down on them. The ratchet handle I am leaning into goes limp when he jumps on my wire. A few turns more and the 35-foot-long, inch-thick cable draws tight again. Steel groans as we tightened wires and snug the six barges closer together.

"Remember boys, the company gives a bonus to any deckhand that can break a wire with a ratchet. Snug 'em up. Get 'em fiddle-string tight. When that pilot steers this tow, I don't want these loads shifting at all!"

When he stopped talking the only sound was the clicking of the ratchets' pawls along the gears of the ratchet barrels. Ratchets are 70-pound turnbuckles that start out seven feet long and tighten down to four feet. They take every inch of slack out of those wires. Sixty or 70 pairs of ratchets and wires will hold 15 loaded barges in a tight unit five barges long by three barges wide. That's a grand total of 1,000 feet by 105 feet. Add the line boat at the stern of the raft, or tow, and a pilot is driving something the size of a ship down a narrow twisting river. It has to be tight or the first hard steer will bust every wire in two.

"C'mon you bums, get them tighter."

I leaned a moment against my cheater bar and took a breather.

After a week out here I had learned many things about towbuilding, but I was also beginning to learn about the characters who people this business. Steamboat Bill was raised in International Falls, Minnesota, but he was born to work on the river. At six feet tall and 180 pounds of solid muscle, he was perfectly built to work the deck of a Mississippi River barge. Square jawed, bearded with twinkling blue eyes, he could have played Paul Bunyan as easily as Mike Fink.

He stopped by my wire a moment. He jumped on it and with a "pop" my handle was loose for another two turns.

"You're scuffin' up those nice new Red Wing boots kid. I warned you about that."

"What do you mean?" I looked down at my boots and wiped at a wad of black grease on the steel toe. Then I wiped the grease from my now well worn White Mule work gloves onto the ratchet handle.

"I told you before, you wear out those boots, and the river will have you. And once she has you, she won't let go. You'll be ruined for any other work but bein' a Mississippi river rat."

I looked at him, took a deep breath and wiped more sweat from my forehead. The smell of the slaughter houses lingered over the river. It was my first week working with these hardened deckhands.

Then he said, getting serious on me, "Look kid this is hard work, and it can be real dangerous, so watch us and don't do anything we don't tell ya to do. And if you're not sure, then just stay out of the way. I am going to expect you to carry your weight around here. They might teach you pilotin' out of a book, but this decking business is strictly hands-on shit!"

I was learning a lot, to be sure. Many of those first lessons were in speaking "deckhand." The nomenclature on the deck of a towboat is unlike that of any other marine endeavor and sometimes seems counterintuitive.

The first language lesson began in my first few minutes of tow building. We were out on those hot barges back in the Pigs Eye Lake fleet wiring up some southbound loads. Bill yelled to me "Hey junior birdman, go cut the cow's-tail on that wire and start layin' it!"

I looked at the coiled wire with an eye pressed into each end and pondered just what the hell he meant. He took in my puzzlement and leaped across the deck to point with his knife.

"See this twine tying the wire into the coil? Cut it!" as he slashed at it with his serrated blade three times cutting three pieces of twine. The wire slithered open. Before it had sprung open all the way, he grabbed the bigger of the two eyes and slapped it over the top of a timberhead on one barge. Then he snatched up the little eye and danced back and forth a couple times around the fittings of the barge butted up to the first. He secured that little eye into the pelican hook of a ratchet, slammed the keeper ring over it and snatched the whole thing tight in the blink of an eye.

"Alright stop standing there and help me hook it. Grab the ratchet in the middle and help me. Slide it forward a bit and then PULL!"

The steel cable jerked up tight, and I leaned into the handle with my knee while he slipped the other pelican hook into a big chain link and forced it shut. He grunted once and forced the other keeper onto that hook.

"Now it's your turn," he pointed at the wire and ratchet for the other side.

I snuck up on the wire and sawed through each wrap of twine — I mean cow's-tail. As I bent down to grab the big eye, one of the loops of wire spun around a kinked spot and whapped me in the forehead. It was like getting hit with a rock. "Ouch!" Steamboat just giggled.

In a matter of seconds I was standing in the middle of the tangled wire trying to get it under control. In each hand I held a part of the length of wire and was trying to hold them apart or pull them together. Pig Man and Sparks came round the corner about then.

"Hey it looks like Junior is getting the hang of it."

"He looks more like Tarzan wrestling a giant python snake to me."

"Yeah, a scrawny Tarzan, 'cause he looks to be gettin' his ass kicked by it!"

Someone must have jumped in and lent me a hand, because in a few minutes we had the wire laid and snatched up to the chain links anchored on the center kevel.

When it was all done, I asked Steamboat "Why do they call it cow's-tail if it's twine? And, for that matter, those lengths of rope — I mean line — you cut up to get it to look like a horse's tail."

"Look kid, you can't change the world from the river. It's always been cow's-tail, it'll always be cow's-tail. It's like towboats. Stupid people who never been out here say, 'why do ya call them towboats? They push. They should be called push boats.' 'No,' I say. 'It goes back to the logging days. Log rafts, when they needed help, got towed by steamboats over bars or around bends. When they first pushed bulk barges of coal, the steamboats were called towboats, and it's towboats today.' Can't change the past from today."

Later he asked me, "What didja think of your first week at solid tow building? Kinduva ball buster ain't it?"

"Yeah, but mostly it's confusing. I mean the fittings on the corners of the barges are all different and some are broken. I still don't get how you lay all those wires. It looks like a big old cat's cradle game to me."

"Uhhuh. That's right. See the trick is to see it all beforehand. Remember, a wire is a stupid thing. Never make a wire do two jobs at once. If a wire is fore and aft, then keep it running straight. If it's a jockey wire, then make sure it stays diagonal between the two barges that are diagonally across, and don't run it to the side of the one butted end on to it. With experience it will get easier." He was using his hands to illustrate these differences for me.

Later I was pushing on a cheater bar with another deckhand to help get the wire real tight. A cheater bar is just a two- to three-inch pipe cut about four or five feet long. It slips over the ratchet handle to put a lot of leverage on a wire.

The wire was tight enough to pluck. I jumped on it one last time. It was as solid as bedrock. I pulled the toothpicks out of the pelican hooks and tapped each one so it wouldn't spin later and cut off someone's toe. Pelican hooks are like clips that open and close to hold the eye of the wire and clip around a set of chain links to anchor the ratchet.

We stepped back and leaned against the bulkhead of the barge to rest a moment before going on to the next chore. As we stepped back, the ratchet exploded. It shot past us and clanged against a steel bulkhead. The dent it put into the three-eighths-inch-thick steel wall was an inch deep. I got up close to the dent and ran my hand over it. A baseball would have fit into it easily. Had it hit either one of us, the most minor injury would have been a crushed bone. Steamboat Bill heard the noise and walked over to see what had happened.

"Didja ever read the label stuck on the barrels of the new ones? They say 'use at your own risk.' Even when the things are used properly, they use a disclaimer. There is just that much force exerted on them. Good thing you weren't next to it." He looked at me, "This is why I say 'Don't straddle the ratchets!'"

"Ouch!" I winced.

"Yeah well, this is break time. We get the big ride all the way to Robert Street fleet. Find a soft spot and take five." He turned and stepped over the splashboard of the towboat *Pawnee.* Then he headed down the port side of the 60-foot boat and disappeared into one of the doors. I took a whiff of the foul air and looked at the greasy deck and wondered what I'd gotten myself into.

Murphy, the pilot, looked down at us while we climbed aboard and threw all our steel tools onto the deck. He shook his head at all the ringing and clanging noise we made just stepping on. He worked the throttles and backed away from the barges in South St Paul and turned the boat towards the airport.

I sat on the bow of the *Pawnee* for a couple more minutes, until the air smelled like we were upwind of the slaughterhouse and stockyards. I followed Bill's path and stood at the bunkroom door looking in at my new crew mates.

"Hey kid, don't wear out that first pair of boots," said a voice from a grimy figure splayed out on a filthy mattress. I looked over at him. His mattress was on a rickety bunk in the dark, dirty bunkroom.

"I told him that already," Bill growled.

"Yeah, besides the most important thing is to get through the first season with all your fingers."

"What do you mean?"

"Well green guys always grab the bight, you know the middle of the face wire, to pull it back and drop over the timberhead to face up."

"Yeah, so do I, so does everyone else." I wasn't sure what he was getting at.

"No, we taught you to grab the wire properly, to the side of the bight like picking up a hula-hoop by the sides and pulling. Some guys put their hands together and pull as hard as they can instead of leaning back into it. As soon as they can squeeze it over the edge they slide it on, and their fingers get pinched between the fitting and the wire. If the pilot loses even the slightest bit of control over the boat — bam! The wire comes tight, he pulls his hand away, and the glove stays behind. Sometimes there is still a finger in the glove."

"Ouch!" I answered.

"Yup, there's probably more guys out here nicknamed three-fingers than anywhere else."

"Well there's Three-finger Lou over at Valley Line," said a third voice.

"There's Three-finger Pete right here in St. Paul," said Bill.

"Yeah, never hurts to count your fingers once in a while kid," said Pig Man.

The boat suddenly rolled and lurched to one side, and I grabbed the door jamb to keep from rolling out into the Mississippi River rolling by.

The voice from inside the dark room was Pig Man, a seasoned deckhand himself. He continued, "Because once you wear out that pair of boots on the deck, you'll be stuck here your whole life like us. She'll get in your blood and you won't be able to get her out."

"I already told him that too," Bill said grinning over at Pig.

I looked about the dingy bunkroom from face to face of my fellow deckhands and blinked. They were a motley looking crew. "I can't believe you guys are layin' on those nasty bunks."

Pig Man opened one eye and drawled, "Why stand when you can sit, and why sit when you can lie. Cripes! It's basic Zen man." Then as he rolled away from me to face the wall. "Just wait man, before long you'll be grateful for these bags to lay on."

As my eyes adjusted to the dim light, I started to wonder if I really wanted to go in there. Grimy, chewed, curled linoleum covered the floor, except where rusty steel deck was exposed in patches. The bulkheads were painted white but caked with soot and grease. Oil and coal dust stained the mattresses of the double bunks lining the forward bulkhead. I stood a safe distance from the bunks myself. Four other deckhands reclined on these fleabag mattresses like kings eyeballing me with equal disdain. I looked out the door at the brown river rushing past and wondered about my new career path. I wondered if I would ever make it as a harbor deckhand. But each day I put in gained me a little more respect from Bill and the crew, and I was beginning to enjoy the work.

Northbound Arrival

About the time we got a southbound tow all wired tightly together, and we thought it was time for a break, we would hear the marine radio over the loudspeaker.

"This is the *Whippoorwill* northbound below Ball Park Bridge standing by for any southbound traffic out of St. Paul."

"*Pawnee* to the *Whippoorwill*. Hey you all got lucky, the Park Bridge tender was awake," Old Murphy would answer.

"Yeah, thank God fer small miracles. Hey ya'll got a home for these empty barges?"

"Bring her on up Cappy. We got a spot for ya right here at the Airport Fleet. Just keep on a comin' 'til ya get shaped up for Pigs Eye Bridge, then take a hard right turn, and we'll be waiting on ya across from Dayton's Bluff."

The line boat pilot was guiding a 1,000-foot-long by 105-foot-wide raft of 15 empties as it eased into the fleeting areas along a bank in South St. Paul. His mate and two deckhands were waiting on the head of the tow. They were rolling up speaker cords and getting the lock lines ready to move over to the southbound tow.

Murph eased the *Pawnee* up to the side of the slowing tow. When the *Pawnee* was next to the head he gently lay against the lead barge and got ready to help push it into the bank. Bill scrambled up the towknee and leapt onto the tow. We three scrambled aboard after him to join the line boat deck crew.

The first order of business was quickly settled. One of the line boat deckhands would ease up to one of us harbor guys and whisper, "Anyone got some pot to sell?"

"No, ah sure don't buddy."

"Damn, I been on this here boat 'bout 45 days and got no relief in sight. Could sure stand a good buzz tonight."

"Sorry pal. Can't help ya."

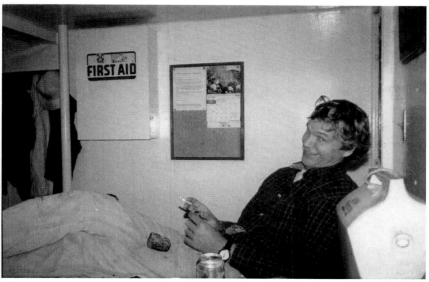

Glenn Carlson relaxes in the galley.

Then the mate would come around the corner to get Bill to walk the tow and count rigging sets. The lonely deckhand straightened up and slid a step away from us. In the background we could hear the pilots' conversation over the loudspeaker and the walkie-talkie on the mate's belt.

"Is our southbound tow ready yet?"

"Yessir. The boys put the pipe to the last set of rigging when you came around the turn back there."

When the head, or bow, of the tow was close to the uppermost piling, Murph would push against the lead empties with the *Pawnee* while the line boat at the stern backed up to stop his headway. We'd line up on the bank side of the bow with our grab hooks and pike poles ready to fish for the anchor wire.

It was a nice easy break in our day. Picking those muck-covered shore wires out of the river bottom and securing the tow with them was the hardest part. Then we got to kick back and smoke cigarettes and sip iced tea in the modern galley of the line boat, while Bill and their mate negotiated a rigging swap. We had to exchange the difference between whatever rigging came northbound and what rigging we'd used to construct their southbound tow.

And that is pretty much the cycle of life in the harbor: land a northbound tow and send them southbound again with 15 loads.

Skylarking

I lasted those first two months and returned to the academy in Helena, Arkansas, where we studied safety rules and practiced laying rigging on cement pads in the middle of a cotton field. Then Twin City Barge brought me back up to St. Paul to rejoin Bill's crew to finish the last two months of the summer. I felt like I was returning home to old friends, and they even treated me like a returning crewmate. The teasing was still there, but it had taken on a different tone. They teased me like a little brother and not a tourist to be pampered and patronized.

Some days the teasing got out of hand. The whole deck crew was standing around on the end of a barge in Red Rock Fleet one morning, when I got tired of it and threw a small fit.

Steamboat laughed at my petulance, and I balled up my fists in anger. He goaded me to "go ahead and take a swing, if you think you're big enough." Finally I took a half-hearted haymaker, which he blocked easily. As he did so, he wrapped me up and carried me like a baby to the bank side of the barge, and without ceremony he deposited me into the muddy water.

"When you're ready to show a little respect and proper manners, I'll pull you out of there."

"Okay," I sputtered, and he reached down and yanked me out of the river with one hand. For the next week I kept my mouth shut, and the teasing tapered off to minor abuse.

Then things took a minor turn, and they began to regard me with a little actual respect. It had come out that the River Academy was a school not just to train deckhands, but also an apprentice pilot training program to meet the demands of a boom industry. Of course when Bill and the gang found out I was part of a steersman program, and it was because my father was connected to the company, they teased me about this new status.

"Hey, I just found out that Junior here is working for free."

"What?"

"He's at that school right? Well he's an apprentice. He works for us for nothing, just the experience."

They all stared at me standing there in the doorway. I looked back at the river behind me, looked for a way out of there gracefully.

"Whaddaya mean you don't get paid? All this tow work, you don't get paid for any of it? Nothing?"

Bill loved this, and the first time we were out building a tow without the *Pawnee*, he brought me into the tiny pilothouse on the tiny tug *Dan Patch*. At times Bill was given command of a smaller boat named the *Dan Patch*, after the famous racehorse from Savage, Minnesota.

The "*Patch*," as we all called her, was only 25 feet long, and the pilothouse was barely 10 feet above the water. Though small, the *Patch* required some amount of skill to pilot, because the boat had only one propeller. There was no "twisting" the engines to turn the boat. The driver had to know where he had room to maneuver and how much room he needed to stop without crashing into a barge.

Bill used the *Patch* to push a small, flat barge full of rigging around the fleets across from the old meat-packing plants of South St. Paul. Most nights we could smell the plant from over the railroad tracks and across the river.

So, when we would use just the small boat alone, Bill would call me up to show me some steering or simply see if I recalled anything from the previous lesson.

"Okay Cubby, show us what you got!" he chided me several times. Then he'd step out of the phone-booth-size pilothouse of the *Dan Patch*. The *Patch*, with 150 hp, was hardly powerful enough to move a loaded barge in a slackwater fleet. She had a wheel to steer with instead of the hydraulic lever most towboats were equipped with.

"Meet us at the next coupling down with the boat," he'd say over his shoulder as he stepped off the boat and onto the barges. He and the boys would disappear down the alley between the strings of barges, leaving me alone on the boat.

When they had reached the next coupling, 200 feet away, they would line up on the outside of the tow to watch. They would laugh and shout advice, as I did circles in the river from trying to land the boat again and getting all out of shape when I backed up on that one rudder.

Out in mid stream I'd spin around trying to get my attitude back and make another attempt to land — spinning the wheel back and forth, shifting the throttle forward and back. RRRRRRR clunk RRRRRR clunk BANG against the barge RRRRRRRR back out into the river. Finally the stern would swing in close enough for Bill to leap aboard. He'd run up the three stairs to the pilothouse. Deftly he'd swing her around and nudge up to the side of the tow.

He chuckled as he walked out and said to me, "Ya know, it's really not that hard."

A Man Overboard Drill

Sometimes even the talented Steamboat Bill had his problems with boat handling. One night we were out on the *Dan Patch* stripping a northbound tow of empties at Packing House Fleet. Packing House was one of three slips cut into the lower end of Pigs Eye Island across the crick from the slaughter houses of South St. Paul.

By 2000 these slips had all silted back in. What's left is visible from Concord Street in South St. Paul as a sand island covered in lush green grass. Back in the 1970s heyday of the harbor, these three slips were still dredged out and held as many as 150 to 200 barges. That is a lot of acres of steel — enough for a little boat to get lost in.

We had the *Patch* pushing a small rigging flat. Bill was running the boat and had a friend with him for the show. Terry Fulton and I were on the deck stringing out wires and stacking ratchets. Bill was working with us and driving the rig between couplings as we finished each one.

The last coupling we had to do was the one closest to where the line boat had been faced up. Called the "steering coupling" it takes the most strain when the big boats steer. The face barge — the one in the middle of the first tier that the boat actually pushes against — had been a load and was already on its way to a terminal in the tow of another harbor tug. Bill was going to put the flat between the two remaining face barges up in the "notch" sort of like driving up into a capital "H." Putting the rigging flat right in the middle of the coupling like that made stripping easier and faster.

The rigging flat slipped easily through the water. On our left the bank of the slip had a muddy stretch of shallow water. Bill snapped on the small searchlight of the *Patch* and swung it around to illuminate the hollow in the tow that he was aiming for. While he adjusted the light to point onto the barges, Bill briefly lit up four pair of eyes low on the muddy bank. Each eye was a fierce red pinpoint. One set was slightly higher than the other three — a mom and three pups. Bill swung the light back off the barges and onto the family of raccoons. One big one and three little ones were busy fiddling with a freshwater mussel.

Raccoons are all over the place down here, they can even climb out onto the barges along the shore wires to get at the spilled grain on the covers and decks. It can be unnerving at night for a deckhand to be walking around in the dark and hear the scrabbling claws on the bare steel.

Terry and I stood on the corners of the flat and signaled Bill towards the notch. Eighty feet away we could hear Bill and his pal yakking and carrying on over the tinny sounding PA system. Terry turned around and grumbled something about Bill paying attention.

Whether he was more distracted by his conversation or the raccoons we never learned.

Soon enough he was yelling out loud at Bill, as we closed on the entrance to the notch. There should have been plenty of room, since the hole was 35 feet wide and the flat was barely 20 feet wide.

"Are you watching my signals? Bill... Bill... Hey Bill!! Bobby grab hold of something quick!" Terry was screaming at the very top of his lungs.

We each got right down on the deck and hugged the timberheads tightly. Before the impact all we heard was Bill say over the faint rock and roll over the PA "I'm backing!"

BOOOOM! Bill nailed the starboard corner of the flat against an empty so hard that I slid completely around the fitting I was wrapped onto. Terry got up off the deck screaming at Bill in the dark.

"Goddammit, when I give a signal would you watch from now on!"

Stepping across the rigging we worked our way back to the boat in time to see Bill pulling himself back through the front window of the pilothouse. A quick assessment of things showed no real damage except for a pile of ratchets that had toppled over. Then somebody noticed that

Bill's buddy was missing. All three of us peered into the night and the river looking for a body. A panic began to grip us, when a muffled sound wafted through the darkness. Together we moved towards the noise.

We stopped at a stack of large truck tires, used to fix shore wires to pilings. Terry shined his flashlight onto a pair of feet sticking out of the pile. We extricated the poor guy from inside the tires. He'd been walking out onto the flat when we'd hit the barges. The impact had hurled him through the air right into the center of the tires.

Murphy's Law and Crossed Signals

Years of hard living gave old Murphy a gaunt look. His long thin hair was flopped over into a kind of a part and his bushy beard looked odd on someone so thin. But all this could not hide the sparkle in his eyes on good days. Clearly, his was a mind that in an easier life would have shone brightly. Old Murphy was the captain of the *Pawnee*.

His job was to shuffle loaded barges around the fleets so that Bill and the boys could wire them up. Each day he showed up carrying a brown-paper-bag lunch that made a noise like a partially drunk bottle when he walked. Between the sticks his boat handling was unconscious. The 60-foot-long 30-ton *Pawnee* became an extension of the old man. He had one rule and one rule only: "Don't screw up!" The boys on deck repeated this often whenever they were doing something on the barges.

Of course my inexperience meant I was constantly breaking that rule and being called on it. For example, later that season I was getting to be more of a help than a hindrance to the other deckhands. I thought I knew all of my hand signals for guiding the pilots from the head of a barge. I'd read them all in a deckhand manual at the academy. Bill and Pig Man decided to put me to the test one night. Old Murphy was building a string of empties for a southbound tow. We'd made a couple of couplings and were shoving three lengths up to yet another empty. It's hard to see out across many hundreds of feet of barge at night. It's even harder to see across the taller empties with a harbor boat some 20 feet shorter than a line boat. These were situations that were likely to trigger Murphy's nasty Irish temper.

Up on top of the fiberglass covers of the barge I gave him my best effort. There I was standing in the spotlight while Murphy was back there in the bag, and the whole thing was going into the toilet. It wasn't long before he was cursing a blue streak at me over the PA. I tried in vain to get him up smoothly to that fourth barge. He just kept backing up, because my signals were either wrong or indistinguishable at that distance. Bill and Pig were down on the line deck getting the rigging ready to hook up in case we ever got close enough to get onto the next barge. They were enjoying the whole thing.

A deckhand waves from atop the pilothouse of the *Patrick Gannaway*.

Pig Man was trying to help me, "Now have him come ahead. Back him now. …all stop. No, no, no! Come ahead again, don't back him so hard…make him twist the head over, hurry, c'mon. What the hell are you doing up there?"

Behind me Murphy screamed over the PA, "What the hell kind of signals are those!?! Did you learn to give those screwed-up signs out of that book? Ah Shit! I don't know what you want!" The exasperated sound of the air valves releasing pressure came over the loudspeaker as the *Pawnee's* engines went all stop.

Pig snickered, "Hey hotshot I thought you knew your signals. Here let me show you." He scrambled up next to me and gave me yet another practical lesson. In seconds he had Murphy touching the barges together as pretty as you please and gentle as eggshells.

Back at the boat Murphy would lean out the window overhead and grin at me, "You know the rule kid. Its real simple. Don't fuck up."

But Murphy never held a grudge and even allowed me to steer the boat for him between fleets. Seated on the lazy bench, he would work on his log book and occasionally glance up to see that I was okay. Usually we were light boat, so it was easy enough and kind of a thrill for a 17-year-old kid to steer a 60-foot, 30-ton boat. One morning he let me steer through Pigs Eye Railroad Bridge in some fog.

The visibility wasn't too bad. The fog was what they call patchy. There would be a thick blinding cloud and then a clear area. Below the bridge we hit a clear spot and a great blue heron glided past the boat. I saw him come up from behind us. The water was glassy smooth ahead of us, and only a couple feet off the surface of the river his wingtips seemed to touch his reflection. He looked like some great water strider. From little fog cloud to fog cloud he had a whole new sky to himself. It occurred to me then that you get to see some pretty cool stuff out here on the river.

A Flash of Insight

There was a moment towards the end of that first season on the river when I knew I was where I was supposed to be. It happened one night while we were stripping the rigging from a northbound tow of coal loads. It was a stormy night, what the men called a real "frog strangler."

In the middle of the downpour I was standing on the edge of one of the barges. Lightning ripped the dark sky, and in that instant I tried to map the deck before me. For a split second, I could see the shiny, rain-slick decks and the other three deckhands dragging rigging. I was dragging a 35-foot wire behind me in each hand. I hesitated a moment longer to judge how far I had to go before I needed to step across the gap between the loads.

They had warned me not to step into the gaps between the barges. One misstep and I would fall into the river and be sucked away by the unforgivable current. No one would see me again, until I was bloated enough to float up from the muddy bottom.

In another flash of lightning I looked down at the flakes of coal dust stuck to my bare legs, arms and chest. Rain gear was no help in this steady downpour, so we'd stripped down to cut-off jeans and steel-toed boots. My steel-toed boots were pretty ragged looking, with a shiny spot where the leather was worn off the toe and the tread worn smooth.

We were nearly done removing all the wire and turnbuckle rigging so that the individual barges could be taken to different parts of the St. Paul harbor. This tow was a raft of Valley Line coal loads tied off to the bank below the Pigs Eye sewage treatment plant.

I was a scrawny snot-nosed kid fresh out of high school, what the other guys called a "green" deckhand. In spite of the reservations I had a couple of months earlier, when I first joined this crew, I was enjoying this work with steel rigging. It was simple work that consisted mainly of knocking ratchets loose, unthreading the wires from around fittings and dragging them across barges to a rigging flat. I looked down and smiled at my nearly worn out boots.

I was pretty satisfied with myself at that moment. I had put on weight and muscle, and I was getting pretty good at helping out the team.

Like a crack of thunder, a voice behind me snapped, "Hey Junior Birdman, get a move on! You're holdin' up the whole friggin' show!" So I put my feet in motion and headed towards the floodlit curtain of rain on the rigging flat. Bill, the fleet mate, snarled impatiently at me through the rain and the darkness. "Standing there daydreaming in the middle of the damn night. I'm soaked and we need to get this tow stripped, so we can get out of this monsoon and get dry. Why are you screwin' the pooch out here? Grab some more rigging and start dragging it onto the damn riggin' flat!"

A voice crackled over the loudspeaker on top of the pilothouse through the rain. It was Murphy's banter and running commentary, which he liked to share whenever deckhands were slaving away. "Well, well, typical deckhands don't have sense enough to come in out of the rain. You guys know the deal. Anyone wants to get out of work can come on up here and take care of me."

"Yeah, yeah," muttered the Pig Man. I didn't want to know what that meant.

Somebody slipped and the sound of chain links clattered on the steel deck. In the darkness Bill cracked wise, "He walks. He talks. He crawls on his belly like a reptile. He's almost human!"

I looked down at the deck in the next flash of lightning, and a thought occurred to me, "Hmmm, I'm going to need a new pair of boots." I wiggled all my fingers in the dark just to check.

From behind me in the dark I heard the clang of metal on metal. A voice barked, "Hey watch out where you're throwin' that."

"Used to be wooden boats and iron men, and now we got wooden men and iron boats," Bill bellowed at us in the dark. "Keep draggin' that riggin'!"

A second voice in the rain retorted, "Iron men my ass!"

Later on we got a change in orders and broke away from Valley Line Fleet to light boat all the way up to the High Bridge Fleet. Murphy leaned out the window, "You clowns might as well take a break. We're going to take the rigging flat up to Robert Street Fleet and strip out an empty tow."

"All right boys, you heard the man. Break time!" said Bill as he led the way back to the bunk room.

"Great, a 40-minute ride," I thought as I settled back onto one of the mattresses in the bunkroom. And then I thought, "This mattress feels pretty damn good."

After my summer learning the craft and science of decking from Steamboat Bill, Twin City Barge assigned me to work the rest of my apprenticeship on a lake boat in Chicago and aboard a line boat on the Tennessee River. When my schooling was complete, they hired me as a steersman in Chicago just in time to lay me off.

The barge towing industry continued to boom through the end of the 1970s. In the middle of this boom TCB dumped all its unionized boat crews and leased their boats out to small, independent operators. So, I was given a short ride to the airport and sent packing to St. Paul.

In St. Paul I began working for a string of these small independent operators. Eventually I landed at the doorstep of Capitol Barge Service.

A Crash Course with
Captain Crunch

"Hey Cap, there's a big log headed your way here!"

I was leaning out over the edge of an empty barge hollering back at the pilothouse atop the towboat *Harry R. Harris*. The towboat was floating in the Mississippi River and tied to the side of a barge moored under the Smith Avenue High Bridge in St. Paul. The empty barge was wired tightly into a raft of fourteen other empty barges newly arrived from St. Louis.

The pilot of the *Harry R. Harris* had many nicknames along the lines of Captain Crunch, but towboaters in St. Paul simply called him Crash. Crash was waiting for us deckhands to turn the barge loose. While we were wrestling one of the outside wires loose I noticed something floating next to the barge. It was going with the current and looked to be on a course for the bow end of the *Harry*.

Crash looked up from the console when he heard me yelling. He had been busily scribbling lies in the boat log. I pointed down at the wooden drift. It was only a few feet long but it was three or four feet in diameter and big enough to possibly make a racket in the propellers.

Distracted by writing in the log, he glanced quickly at where I was pointing and saw nothing.

"Listen here you punk kid, when I want lip from you I'll let ya know!"

"But," I pointed again at the huge stump floating like an iceberg below the surface of the water.

"Get your ass back to work and stop wasting my time!"

I shrugged my shoulders and slunk back around to the end of the barge and continued to gather up loose rigging, wires, ratchets and chain links.

In a few minutes the older deckhand who was training me, Senator, walked to the edge of the barge and raised both hands straight into the air. "All gone!" he yelled at Crash.

We watched as Crash stood between the rudder tillers and began to move the main engine ship-ups. The stern of the boat swung out away from the barge slowly. He backed hard into the deck line. With a groan the thick polypropylene rope came tight, and the bow of the boat dipped down from the strain. With a sickening squeak, the empty we were on began to slide out from between the other barges still wired hard together.

Over the squealing and grinding of steel on steel as the empty barge began to slide past the other empties, we heard a nasty "clunk."

Crash screeched over the loudspeaker, "Catch me a line. Tie this barge off! I've got something caught in the wheels!"

Senator and I stood out on the end of the barge now floating free. "Guess he should've listened to your punk ass, huh Junior?" he chuckled softly.

Three hours later the towboat *Harry R. Harris* was moored alongside the wharf barge under the Smith Avenue High Bridge waiting for a diver to come and clear a large obstruction that had lodged between the propellers. Crash and I sat across from each other on empty wooden spools used to ship inch-and-a-half steel cable. He was really mad because the diver was our boss Draine-O. The boss had to cut his vacation on Madeline Island, in Lake Superior, short to fly back and get us running again.

Crash glared at me, as steam rolled out of his ears. He couldn't say anything to me, but somehow he felt I was to blame. Crash was a big guy who I didn't want mad at me. He had solid, square features under thick curly black hair. Over his snarling lips he had a thick black mustache. His temples were throbbing, and his huge forearms flexed anxiously. He was as strong as a gorilla and nearly as smart.

I was beginning to suspect that Crash was a bit unbalanced. As time went on, I learned that he had a tragic flaw that made piloting on the river a bad choice for him. The river had gotten to him and was working on his weaknesses. Crash's main weakness was that he had the personality of Wolf Larsen, the domineering captain in Jack London's novel *The Sea-Wolf*, and the luck of Curly from the Three Stooges. I had the bad luck to be working for him during the seasons when his luck really took a nasty turn.

Bob Draine works between the sticks of the *Harry R. Harris*.

A good sea story always has a maniacal character for an antagonist and mine is no different. In many maritime tales there is a character with a flaw that takes him to the brink of madness. There are many examples like Queeg and Ahab who dragged the whole crew down with them. In *Life on the Mississippi* Mark Twain wrote of a pilot named Brown, whose nature was so vile he drove a young Twain to violence.

But during the two seasons I worked for Twin City Barge, the Mississippi became my home and many of the rough and crude rivermen came to treat me like an annoying younger brother. For a kid who had grown up moving from Air Force base to Air Force base every year, the shifting river gave me stability. But my home on the river was about to lose its foundation in the turbulent waters of an unstable captain.

When TCB was forced to close its marine operations, I headed back to St. Paul to look for deckhand work. A half dozen one- and two-boat operators rushed to fill the void that TCB had left. I landed a deckhand job with the best of these small operators. Bob Draine, who the St. Paul rivermen simply called Draine-O, was the owner-operator-engineer of his Capitol Barge Service. His were the red and white boats tied under the old Smith Avenue High Bridge for nearly 30 years. These four small towboats — the *Harry R. Harris* (called the Weird One), the *Lois E* (named for his mother), the little *Arlene* and his flagship, the mighty *Mike Harris* — were his pride and joy.

Draine-O and his Capitol Idea

Draine-O had another connection to me. He and my dad were buddies. Dad flew the executive plane for the Twin City Barge muckymucks, and Draine-O had some tight business ties with TCB.

As an upshot of this tie, Dad and Draine-O spent a considerable amount of time flying around the Midwest in the company plane together. When Draine-O hired me, he concluded the interview by telling me a story about one of their trips.

"One time we were flying south, and our flight path took us over some farmland in Kansas. I made the mistake of telling your dad that 'I sure would like to see what it's like to fly low once.'"

"Buckle up Bucko!" Dad responded, and he put that MU-2 into a steep dive.

"I grabbed ahold of that seat cushion and damn near ripped it off the floor. Next thing I know we're looking eyeball to eyeball with a farmer on a tractor and haystacks are goin' right by the window, and I say to your dad, 'I hope none of those farmers report us to the FAA.'"

"He says to me, 'Don't worry. We are going way too fast for them to see the ID numbers on the plane, and the Feds will think he saw a UFO anyway!'"

He loved flying on the edge. One of the lessons he taught me was how to perform a loop the loop. When Dad skipped town he went south to fly crop-dusters over cotton fields in the Mississippi Delta. The only airplane crash he ever had was when a Grumman Ag-Cat he was flying was sabotaged by a white farmer who resented his drinking after work with the black field hands.

After the old man skipped town, Draine-O felt he wanted to help me out. He hired me on the spot to fill a deckhand position on one of his red and white towboats.

That sense of caring, or whatever it was, did not preclude sticking me with a lunatic. He had a pilot who entered the pilothouse in middle age, too late to handle the rigors of working the St. Paul harbor. Most harbor tugs handle a few terminals along a stretch of the river and service tows as they pass northbound and southbound. In St. Paul and Minneapolis pilots have a more demanding job. They have to be able to switch elevators, run the locks of Minneapolis and deal with the twisting bends of the Minnesota River, in addition to assisting tows in and out of St. Paul.

Old timers like to describe piloting on the river as being "90 percent pure boredom and 10 percent sheer terror." Well, Draine-O's pilot would have preferred those odds because to him it was 110 percent terror, and I was assigned to him for two years. They were two of the most challenging years of my life.

Some form of madness strikes many riverboat pilots. Whatever character flaw a man has will be exposed and intensified between the sticks in a pilothouse. Paranoia, megalomania, misplaced and projected anger, whatever is in there will come out like parasites in the brain and spill out onto the deck and infect the whole crew.

Old Man River can do the same things to a man's soul that he does to the landscape. The same currents that carve up banks and uproot trees will cut into a weak man's soul and twist it around until it is unrecognizable. I saw up close how the river can take a man's flaws and use them to twist his luck, darken his soul and completely break him down.

Ghosts and Demons

"Captain Crunch" hated his nickname but knew that he was stuck with it. It was a moniker that he earned the honest way. It happened one day, as he was southbound through downtown Minneapolis and had a nasty accident. The zigzags at Nicollet Island got him. A tricky little set of steers must be performed alongside of Nicollet Island on the approach to the Upper St. Anthony Falls Lock chamber.

Before the new Hennepin Avenue Bridge was built, in 1988, there was a pier in the middle of the river. So when a barge pilot would come downstream into the lock at the Upper St. Anthony Falls Dam, he had to steer way over onto the bank at Nicollet Island to get under the Great Northern Railroad Bridge then cut across to the opposite side of the river to get into the lock chamber.

People used to watch this tricky steer from both sides of the river. We deckhands would see all the old mansions of the island from practically their front yards and then be close enough on the other side to talk with the bums sleeping under the old Post Office.

One of his first times coming through Crash over steered bad enough to nearly drive a coal load right into the Post Office. He tore out a hundred feet of wooden guard fencing surrounding the land-side pier, and he put a hole big enough to drive a car through in the lead barge.

For weeks that year the barge sat in a fleet in South St. Paul with that huge tear in the rake end. Some joker noticed something familiar in the shape of the tear. One night he snuck out to the fleet in a small boat and painted teeth and lips around it. Local river rats began to call it Crash's "shark" barge.

It only took one mistake to earn the nickname, but he renewed it on a daily basis. He never regained his nerve, and the ghosts and demons that haunted his dreams after the accident caused him to twitch and jerk, even when he was awake. He was forever after convinced that the river conspired against him.

These demons of his took many traditional forms, but his main bugaboo was driftwood. Logs, snags, anything that floated and even the occasional uprooted tree found its way into the propellers and rudders of his vessel. He had some sort of weird alchemy with organic objects. Anything floating in the river that had leaves or had at one time been covered in leaves was somehow attracted to his steel propellers. This power was not without a price. Each time he used it, he took a step closer to the brink of madness.

I got a glimpse of his particular brand of madness one of the first nights I decked for him. We had departed the barge fleet under the Smith Avenue High Bridge and were pushing a tow of four empty barges up the Minnesota River to Savage. It was getting near to midnight, and a gentle spring shower had quickly turned into a thunderstorm.

I climbed up to the pilothouse and settled into the red cushioned lazy bench behind the pilot's chair. Silhouetted against the front window Crash had his hands on the steering sticks. Every few seconds he'd lift the one with a cigarette perched between his fingers to his lips. It glowed bright red for an instant, and he'd set it down in the ashtray. He'd set it right next to the other one that was still lit.

The sappiest country music ever recorded was dripping from his cheap radio. After a minute he fumbled in the dark for his cigarette pack and lit a third one. I heard the sound of his nerves fraying. It sounded like a banjo string tightening. There was faint rise in pitch, and then it snapped with a "twang!"

"Deckster, I need ya to ride the head and watch for pleasure boats for me. They're thick tonight!"

I turned to peer out the window. The raindrops slanting past the window were catching red and green reflections from the running lights on the pilothouse. I sighed and stifled the urge to inform this genius that no one in their right mind was on the river in this foul weather. Instead I said, "Okay Cap. Gimme a minnit to put on my rain gear, and I'll head right out."

The rain seemed to come down harder with every step I took towards the head of the tow. A thick lock line was lying loose on the steel deck. Dragging it over to the bulkhead, I coiled it under the two-foot overhang of the barge covers. I took one more look back to the boat. Crash had each searchlight swinging back and forth across the barge covers and bank to bank. The round beams illuminated the raindrops, so that they looked like the spherical glittering explosions of a fireworks show. With a sigh I wrapped my raincoat tightly around myself and settled down on the coiled line for a wet nap. The walkie-talkie lay on the deck next to my head.

Crash's voice came over the speaker, "Whaddya see Deckster?"

"No pleasure craft out here tonight, Cap."

"Okay, uh… is there any stumps floatin' down, can ya tell?" The beams from his twin searchlights crossed and crisscrossed ahead of the tow.

"Yeah, uhhuh, okay yeah that's good. Nope. Don't see nuthin' but dark, Cap."

I rolled over and got back to my nap, but I couldn't really sleep, so I just sort of closed my eyes between thunder claps. The tow was coming up on Four-Mile Cut.

Four-Mile Cut is that stretch of river between the airport and Cedar Avenue Bridge. The bottom wetlands stretch away for a mile on either side of the main channel. The elms and cottonwoods lined both sides of the river with their bare branches spread out against the darkness. Each bolt of lightning illuminated a surreal scene. I imagined the trees to be a band of wild beings running around with their hands in the air. Back in the pilothouse, Crash saw only goblins waiting to fall into the river and get sucked into his propellers.

Then there was something in the river ahead of us, but it wasn't a tree floating loose. I waited for another flash of lightning to see what it was. It was a big buck deer with a rack like a tree. He was swimming across the channel ahead of the tow. No sense in alarming Crash with this tidbit, so

I just watched as the beast clambered up the steep bank. On top of the levee he turned to look at the dark apparition that had chased him from the river. It was as if he was staring right at me. Then he turned and casually walked into the woods.

"Well at least we won't get any drift caught under the boat tonight."

That night we didn't get any driftwood caught in the rudders or propellers, but later we would gather more wood than a team of lumberjacks. And when Senator became Crash's lead man and my supervisor, everything that happened to Crash turned into a big practical joke. And at first he was a buffer between me and Crash's bad temper.

Senator

The door between the galley and the engine room banged open, and a cloud of steam rolled over me. The whine of the turbochargers and the din from all three main engines of the *Harry R. Harris* overwhelmed my senses. From within the cloud, an apparition appeared: Senator himself ascended from the bowels of the boat.

He closed the door and removed his earphones. His thin reddish hair was matted to his skull with sweat. He was rail thin and shirtless. His middle-aged skin was losing its elasticity.

He had been down in the engine room — where it's just about 180 degrees — using a pressure washer on the main engines. It made for a miserable sauna, but it kept the oil and grease off of the engines. He wasn't about to let those engines get dirty or oily, not since the night the *Harry R. Harris* burned up.

Around midnight on a hot August night in 1975, one of the many hydraulic hoses between the gearbox and the main engine blew, spraying hydraulic fluid all over a cherry-red-hot turbo, setting the boat on fire. It happened between Watergate Marina and Hidden Falls, right under the parapets of old Fort Snelling. Senator was walking down the narrow gunwale next to an engine room window, when one of the engines exploded, throwing him into the river.

Luckily he landed draped over one of the boat's face wires, which connect the vessel to the barges. The other deckhand heard the explosion and happened onto the scene in time to catch Senator before he slipped into the river and under the boat, where he would surely have gotten chopped up by the propellers.

Later, when Bob Draine, the owner of the company, and the fire marshal were standing on the head deck surveying the damage, a fire axe suddenly thrust its way between them through the splintering glass of the galley window. The embarrassed helmeted face of a the firemen appeared and sheepishly whispered "Sorry Chief. Ventilation ya know," and quickly disappeared.

When the insurance company handed him a check, Draine went straight away to the Allis-Chalmers Diesel Company, and, as it was the Bicentennial year of 1976, he was told he had a choice of engine block colors. He chose red, white and blue. So that year the *Harry* was powered by three main engines in the colors of our nation's flag. Senator took a lot of pride in these mains and wasn't about to let them get dirty.

As he stepped to the refrigerator he wiped his horn rimmed glasses with a shop rag pulled from a back pocket. He opened the door and withdrew an opaque plastic pitcher. He held it up at eye level and then looked to me with an accusing eye.

"You didn't drink any of my Kool-Aid, didja Junior?"

Then he took a huge swig and wiped his mouth with the back of his hand.

"Well I better go check on that pussy, Crash. Gotta make sure he ain't wetting his pants over some pleasure boat or log floatin' down the river."

"Kids!" he spat my way over his shoulder as he left the galley to climb the stairs to the pilothouse. "They keep hiring kids to work out here. What do effing kids know about work?"

Senator was the old man of the deck crew at Capitol Barge Service. He was showing me the ropes of working the harbor between St. Paul and Savage, up on the Minnesota River, and taking barges through the St. Anthony locks up in Minneapolis. His temperament was acidic, and his view of me was jaundiced. Still, he liked something about me and was trying his best to be patient with me and raise me right.

Later, when I was standing on the stern of the boat watching the steering ram wiggle back and forth as Crash steered down the river, I saw something strange out of the corner of my eye: A glass bottle flew from the front of the boat where Senator was into the back of the barge we were pushing and broke into a thousand pieces that fell into the river.

Senator had a mean streak that played into his sense of humor. One morning Crash had a barge shoved up against a cluster of pilings. Each piling is a steel pipe over a foot in diameter. When a dozen of them are driven into the mud bottom and wrapped tightly together with cable, they make a structure strong enough to tie many tons of loaded barges to.

Getting a thick rope around them can be a challenge, since they seem to be as thick as a redwood trunk when a deckhand is trying to get his arms around them. The easiest way is to swing a length of the rope at the eye end to the back of the piling and then try to catch it with your other hand when it comes around the other side.

It is a lot easier with two sets of hands. He would swing the eye end of the rope around to the back of the pilings, and I would reach out to catch it. We tried this a time or two, and the rope splashed into the river. I reached out a little farther, and the throw seemed to come up even shorter. So I reached out more, teetering precariously on the edge of the barge. I lunged for the elusive eye and went head first into the river. The pilings set off the bank 20 to 30 feet, so I wasn't out in the current. It was a dry year, so there wasn't much current to begin with. But the water is just as wet in a flood year as a drought, so I came up sputtering and soaked all the same.

When I was up on the deck dripping wet, he began to chuckle at me. I looked at him closely. Did he really just pull the rope away from me as I was about to grab it?

The next time it happened, I knew for sure he was doing it on purpose. There was no danger of me getting hurt, because the barges were at a standstill, but still I was learning that his sense of humor — his idea of a practical joke — was a bit sadistic.

Red Flag Rising

One morning in mid June our day started as so many did when Crash was piloting, with the general alarm bell going berserk. The water was down from the spring flooding, so that couldn't have been what had him panicked. Senator followed me out the galley door onto the head deck of the *Mike Harris*.

A couple of empty barges were in tow ahead of the boat. We were on the way from the empty barge fleeting above the I-35W Bridge to the grain docks in Savage. The most immediate problem was that Crash had the barges pointed to a spot somewhere beyond the tree-lined bank up into the hills of Bloomington.

Senator yelled up, "What's wrong now, Crash?"

"Hurry up and knock me out! I've got some drift under the boat!"

I felt a gentle tug on my sleeve. Senator was standing on the head deck to where he could see down the length of old Mike. Leaning over I saw what he was pointing at. There was a whole tree sticking out of the back end of the boat, and it was caught underneath in the rudders and propellers.

We scurried up the Mike's narrow tow knees and proceeded to take off the face wires. Normal procedure dictates that if possible a pilot should attempt to secure his tow in an emergency, and as we were right next to TCB's Credit River Empty Fleet, we could have. We knocked the boat out of tow, all the while Crash was yelling at us to hurry and glancing back towards the stern as if it were about to explode.

"Get your pike pole and stand by back there, while I try to get that drift loose."

I went to the hooks on the side of the boat and wrestled the 20-foot-long aluminum pole from its saddle. These poles have a small pike and hook on one end for prodding and pulling drift and dead things away from the barges, or sometimes, just for retrieving baseball caps blown off a head.

The *Mike Harris* at the wharf barge under the old Smith Avenue High Bridge.

So we went back and set on the stern, while Crash did doughnuts in the water and our barges, being empty and in pool water, sailed on up the river gradually losing their point. He steered hard on the boat. He twisted her around one way and another, using the engines one forward and one in reverse as a tractor would.

Nothing worked. Finally he stepped out the door of the pilothouse and took a good long look at the tree still jutting out gaily from under the stern between the rudders and the wheels. Senator and I looked at Crash, then at the tree, then at each other, then up river past Crash at our empties as they rammed into the bank.

"Boom! Snap!" Another tree fell over and halfway into the river. Crash jerked around, and when he saw the empties gently topping in the river coming back downstream at us, he grabbed a hunk of his hair and began to pull. Now he was absolutely beet red in the face.

Something in him snapped when he realized we were sitting there calmly in the face of his present disaster. "Lean on that damn pole and see if you can shove that tree out of there."

Pike poles typically have a pointed tip twisted like a cork screw for just such an occasion.

Senator shook his head as he stood. "Okay rookie jab her in there somewhere, and let's pretend this might work."

Pushing as hard as we could did nothing to dislodge that tree. Crash looked back and forth from where we were working on the tree under the boat to the loose barges headed for the tree line of the bank ahead. Jumping back inside the wheelhouse he jammed the throttles in gear. I don't know if he came ahead or astern. All I remember is that the pole jerked out of our hands and almost pulled us over the side. At the same time it came loose from the tree, then regaining our balance one of us grabbed for the pole before it fell. Senator put the pole on the deck and told me to "Sit down for a minute, while I go tell Crash to warn us before he uses those damn engines again."

Crash was still jockeying the engines back and forth, so I never heard what Senator yelled at him. When he came back to the stern red-faced and shaking his head some more he said, "Look, Crash wants you to go find a piece of cow's-tail and a red rag to tie on the branch there so he can see it."

I looked skeptically at that tree limb sticking out of the water a few feet off the side of the boat. "What?"

"I know. I know. It sounds crazy, but he wants to be able to see it move from up there."

Looking from that tree branch up to Crash on the wing of the pilot-house, I thought to myself, "Well this isn't the stupidest thing he's ever requested." On the head deck I leaned into one of the tow knees and got a two-foot-long piece of cow's-tail and rummaged around the shackles and chain links for a piece of red rag.

There wasn't a rag to be had on the head deck, and I headed into the galley and engine room for it. I went straight for the box in which Senator kept his supply of red shop rags.

I turned around and bolted back through the alley to the head deck. The main engines continued going from full ahead to full astern, and the boat rumbled fiercely as the tree was being pounded up against the hull.

I looked up at the pilothouse, when Crash leaned out the window. He kept shifting the engine throttles while he yelled at me, "Where the hell have you been?" Just then the tree jerked and come out a few feet.

Holding up the rag and twine for him to see, I asked, "Do you still want a flag on it?"

His face immediately turned crimson and spit flew from his mouth. "Why you stupid little sunnavabich! What do you mean 'put a flag on it!?'"

I started to shake with fear and confusion. I sputtered, "B-b-b-but you told Senator." My voice faltered as I noticed back at the stern of the boat Senator was wearing a wide grin. He'd got us both good. In another few seconds the tree rumbled free of the boat, and we raced to regain control of our empty barges. Senator wore that grin all day long, and Crash rode me like a drill sergeant the rest of the day.

Action on the Poop Deck

Crash was steering past the St. Paul Pool and Yacht Club coming up on the I-35E Bridge about a half mile below the mouth of the Minnesota River. Yacht Club members were seated at the tables stretched out along the veranda. They were maybe wondering what it was like to spend a life on the river, while Steamboat Bill and I wondered how that cold beer must taste on such a nice day from their lookout. The wooden cigar-store Indian next to the brass bell was thinking nothing but how stiff he must be.

The water was sparkling brightly, and the sun was warm on my face. Pleasure boats were out in force zipping up and down the river making their graceful arcing swoops towards the barges as they passed. Steamboat and I were reclined on the curved fiberglass covers of four empty barges heading for Savage.

To our right was Crosby Lake Park, and to our left was a steep embankment that had a train track cut into it. Off in the distance we could see old Fort Snelling. The old fort sits high above the tree line that is Pike Island. Seeing it from this vantage always made me wonder about what it must have been like to live here a hundred years ago, when settlers were just moving in and the Minnesota River Valley was occupied by a few farmers and the Indians.

"HONK!" Crash gave a short toot on the powerful cluster of Kahlenberg horns that Draine-O had on the *Mike Harris*.

Steamboat and I walked to the opposite sides of the tow to see if some small boat had buzzed him too closely. We looked at each other, shrugged our shoulders and returned to our spots on the cover.

"That Crash is sure a nervous cat when the pleasure boats are out," snorted Steamboat. We resumed our girl watching.

Disdainful of modern technology, Draine-O had not yet outfitted the deck crews with walkie-talkies. We were left with using hand signals to communicate with the pilot. Bill lazily lifted his hand in the air and gave his middle finger in the general direction of Crash.

"HONK! HONK!"

"What the hell is wrong with him?" Steamboat snapped.

Empty barges only draw about two feet of water, but they are 15 to 20 feet high, depending on the style of covers. This makes it tricky to drive them with the *Mike Harris*, as her pilothouse has only 22 feet for height of eye. With four empties you look across a field of fiberglass 70 feet wide and 400 feet long at eye level to navigate. This makes it difficult to see small boats that constantly play chicken with the tow. Steamboat and I figured that Crash, who was deathly afraid of pleasure boats anyway, was just having one of his attacks.

We looked around the inside corner of the barges where they were breasted together and down the alley where we could see the pilothouse. Crash was motioning us back and was ready to blow the horn again.

"That chickenshit prick! He wants someone to hold his hand or make him a pot of coffee!" Steamboat Bill shook his head.

I slid forward on the cover and hopped to my feet. Steamboat put his hand to my shoulder. "Leave him be. For crying out loud. We finally get a break, and he can't stand to see us relax for a half hour."

So I sat back down. Leaning back against the cover, I closed my eyes and felt the warm sun sweep over my face.

"HONK! HONK! HONK! HONK!"

Four short blasts did not mean coffee time. It was a danger signal. Though Crash was always the first to panic, still we were obligated to respond to that one.

Opening my eyes to see trees sweeping across the deck towards me, I rolled quickly to the right towards the alley and off the covers. Steamboat grabbed my arm and pulled me into the alley and safety from the tree limbs that were snapping and scraping on the covers, lifting them off of the hopper coamings as the tow slid into the bank and under the overhanging tree branches.

We quickly went into that hurry-up gait used by barge hands in an emergency. It's a kind of race walk gait with a wiggle thrown in every couple of seconds to dodge the shin high horns of the kevels along the sides of the barge. One misstep provides a bone-crunching reminder to practice that wiggle with your legs.

"Do ya think it's a real emergency Bill?"

"If it is, the damn fool scared himself to death over somethin'."

"Geez, could he of had a heart attack?"

"Ooooh a heart attack. Naw, the prick doesn't have a heart. Who knows, he probably spilled some coffee and didn't know whether to wipe or steer, and his brain froze up from the confusion of it all."

We scurried back to the face of the tow and started to clamber over the towknees. The sound of Crash cussing at us prompted me to look up. He was out of the wheelhouse and coming down the steps leading to the head deck. In one hand he held aloft a pair of soiled boxer shorts and in the other his jeans, only the tails of his western-style shirt covered his nakedness.

"Didn't you hear me blowin' the damn whistle? I had to take a shit! I waited too gawddam long and crapped in my drawers!"

Bill retorted, "Well Crash, it figures you were so full of crap it had to spill out sooner or later!"

Crash glared at us. "You guys better not ever tell anyone about this!"

As he turned at the foot of the stairs to go into the galley, a gust of wind caught his shirttail and lifted it up to reveal the scene of the crime and the mess thereon.

"Ohmygawd — I could have gone all day without seeing that!" I gagged and turned away.

Steamboat turned his head away at the same time. "How will I get to sleep tonight?"

For weeks afterwards someone would occasionally sneak a disposable diaper into his lunchbox, and Crash would glare at me as if I had done it.

A Shock in the Dark

Of course things didn't always turn out better when I did steer for him. One nasty night I was sitting in the galley of the *Harry R. Harris* when the call buzzer sounded. Walking out to go upstairs, I stepped into the middle of a spring downpour. Bracing myself against the wind, I made my way back to the stairs leading up to the pilothouse.

Once inside Crash said without looking at me "Here, take her. I need to fix something."

As I stepped between the sticks he squatted beside me and opened the breaker cover for the port searchlight.

I turned my attention to the two empties ahead of me. The *Harry R. Harris* was even shorter than the *Mike* by a couple of feet. We were up bound by the airport in St. Paul, so I could steer by looking up at the navigation lights of the Lafayette Bridge. The wind was blowing so hard that in order to steer up through the middle of the bridge span the barges had to be pointed directly at the bridge pier itself.

I chanced a glance down at Crash. He was on his knees at my side with his sleeves rolled up. In one hand he had a butter knife and in the other a rubber handled screwdriver. Elbows up in the air he had his huge hands and these utensils stuffed into the breaker box trying to get that port light working. Then I noticed that he was holding that rubber handled screwdriver down by the head, and I worried that with the butter knife in his other hand he just might at some point complete the circuit with himself.

"Uuuhh, Captain do you think that's a good idea to do that like that? Couldn't you get electrocuted?"

He pulled his hands out and shook the butter knife in my face menacingly. "Listen here, I don't need any advice from a smart-assed kid. Now just you steer this boat like I told you!" With that he turned and jammed his hands back into his work. Thoroughly chastised, I peered back into the slanting rain and never looked at him again.

A minute later I heard a snap and smelled something burn. This was accompanied by a strained sort of groan, "Uuunnnnggghhhh!"

I looked in time to see Crash fly back onto the lazy bench. He lay there spread eagle and shuddered a few times from head to foot. Moving the chair out of my way I stepped towards him to see if he was okay. When I turned on the overhead light, I could see the dark stain spreading in the crotch of his pants.

A moment later, when he had recovered somewhat, he turned the light off and stepped to the door.

"Um you hold her a while longer, whilst I go wash my hands."

I was barely able to hold my laugh until he was safely out of hearing. On his return he dismissed me saying "You better not ever tell anyone about this!"

So the next day when I was telling another deckhand, named Turbo, about the incident, he laughed and said, "Yeah, he did the same thing last winter, when we were rebuilding the main engines on the *Mike*. He was shoved under the oil pan of the center engine fiddling with the starter wiring or the fuel solenoid — I can't remember. But he was layin' there, and all I could see was him from the waist down sticking out of there. All of a sudden his legs jerked a couple times, and he moaned real low and hard. Then his legs sort of relaxed, and his pants were just soaked."

The Sky is Falling!

There were other occasions when Crash got a chance to get the whole harbor on high alert status with his inability to respond appropriately to emergencies. One night I was an unwilling accomplice in one such affair.

We'd been downbound out of Savage on the *Harry* with our usual four loads. I'd done all my duties in the engine room and had stepped back on the stern to cool off and have a smoke.

There is a sound that iron propellers make working away beneath the steel hull. It is a sort of "whooshing" sound. The whooshing is punctuated by the wiggle and squeal of the hydraulic system moving the rudders back and forth against the force of the wheel wash.

We were coming down on Omaha Railroad Bridge and I had a nice view of downtown St. Paul at night. There was the First Bank red "1" all lit up. The stars were bright. I lifted my head to take it all in.

I felt some moisture on my head. "That's funny it's sprinkling, but the sky is absolutely clear?!" Then I thought it must be my imagination because it seemed to stop.

Then I felt some moisture sprinkle my head again. "Hmmmnn, what's going on?"

Then it stopped again.

After a half minute I realized that every time the stern shifted — that is whenever Crash steered — it sprinkled. I turned on my flashlight and began examining the steering hoses and rams under the grate. Sure enough, there was a pinhole leak on one of the hydraulic hoses.

I watched it a few times and then ducked into the engine room and looked at the hydraulic tank. Still mostly full, thank goodness it's a slow leak. We had time to get to fleet before we had to panic — plenty of time to do a repair in a quiet setting.

When I told Crash, he decided it called for a full-blown emergency call. He backed up and stopped our tow in the bridge span.

"How bad is the leak?"

"I don't know. It's leaking. Spraying straight up into the air."

"Well do I have enough steering to get down to the fleet?"

"I don't know. You could stop right over there at High Bridge Fleet."

"Do I have enough steering to get there? C'mon you're the utility man. Do I have steering until then?"

The *Mike Harris* passes through the Omaha Railroad Bridge with six loads. (photo by Brian Brezinka)

I looked down the river a thousand feet to where the High Bridge was. Any other pilot would just start backing in, but Crash wanted me on the hook for his decision. Technically I couldn't say for certain that the fluid in the reservoir would last another five minutes, though I knew that it probably would.

"I don't know, but I think it should."

I could hear the pores in his skin stretch open with a creak and begin to ooze ice-cold sweat. Crash reached for the marine radio.

Within an hour every spare tug in the immediate area was tearing our tow apart to deliver to terminals and haul us down to the wharf barge. The 30-gallon tank had leaked barely a gallon of fluid.

Pine-Sol Sabotage

Crash got carried away with a lot of mundane things as well — things as mindless as housekeeping. He expected the wheelhouse to be kept spotless. The *Harry* had a small wheelhouse, as did most of the harbor tugs, and it was in dire need of remodeling. Draine-O, for all his boat wisdom, had a thing for red. His boats — the *Harry*, *Mike*, *Lois E* and *Arlene* — were each painted red and white on the inside as well as the outside. Keeping the boats sparkling was a big part of a deckhand's duty.

Well the *Harry* had the ugliest, darkest shade of red paint on her pilothouse walls. The console was also red, solid red broken up only by the chrome tiller sticks and the brass controls for the searchlights. Keeping these things clean wasn't too terribly difficult. One just wiped and polished them down daily. The floor was another matter. When the boat had been refurbished after a fire in 1975, everything was brand new. Three years later, when I was the deckhand, things were beginning to show considerable wear. The floor was a curled up, yellowed, cracked and disintegrating grid of linoleum squares. It was worn practically through in the center, where the pilot's chair was continually moved around as the pilots performed their many duties, day in and day out.

No matter, Crash expected it to be kept clean, nay, immaculate. As for any other pilot on any other watch or boat, I swept and mopped it daily. Not good enough, oh no. Crash expressed his wish that I scrub it on my hands and knees with Comet cleanser after sweeping, and only then could I mop. It wasn't such a huge directive in and of itself, but a deckhand has a fairly full 12-hour schedule. There was tow work at the beginning and end of several runs daily, in addition to the deck maintenance, rope splicing, keeping the lower cabins neat and cleaning the outside of the boat, especially the head deck, where we had be able to move around and find things fast when things were hopping.

One morning I was washing down the walls in the pilothouse.

"Hey, you missed a spot here. Not there. Fer Gawds sake can't you scrub any better than that!?"

"Whaddaya mean? That's clean!"

"It's not good enough!" he said wiping his finger across a cigarette film in one of the ceiling corners.

"Hey it's hard to be that careful on every damn spot."

"Hey it's hard for me to scrub my balls when I take a shower, but I do it!"

Jerking the bucket off the floor, I got out of the pilothouse fast.

I went into the galley where Senator was looking through the newspaper. He looked up at me and cocked his head. He must have seen something on my face. "What's wrong with you?"

"I just got my ass chewed out because Crash's balls are hard to scrub."

We were getting used to his craziness, because Senator simply said "oh" and went back to his paper. I reached under the counter and grabbed a large bottle from under the sink drain.

"We're going to need a lot more of this," I said as I poured the entire contents of the bottle into a bucket of hot water. A green cloud and the smell of a million pine trees filled the galley.

"Get that stinkin' shit outta here!"

"Oh I will." I headed right back up to the pilothouse. I began a campaign to make sure he never mentioned his ball-washing to me again!

My cleaning the floor and walls properly became his pet peeve. And mine. It was starting to eat larger and larger chunks of my time every day. Senator would just shake his head when that bell rang as soon as we were settled down for a coffee break fresh off the tow. "Yup, it's time to clean his damn floor. Better get moving."

I'd drag myself up to the pilothouse with my broom, mop and bucket with rag and scoring pad. When I discovered the sinus clearing strength of Pine-Sol, my life became easier. Oh, I still had to put in extra time on the floor, but it was so rewarding to listen to Crash whine and snivel about how strong that stuff was: "Geezus Deckster, do you have to mix it so strong? It's hurting my eyes, and I can barely breathe!"

"But Crash, it's the only thing that gets that grease and dirt off!" I could have been a Pine-Sol commercial on television.

I'd stand back and gaze lovingly at the floor and swoon a bit. He didn't have the nerve to tell me to quit doing something that he'd made such a grand deal out of. Then I'd sit back and watch Crash rub his eyes for a good 40 minutes or so.

Out on deck, later in the day, I could look back to the boat and see him shove his head out the open door and take a big suck of the breeze blowing by the pilothouse.

"Nuthin' like a breath of fresh air," I'd whisper to myself, smiling.

Where There's Smoke

When I started decking in St. Paul, Draine-O still used red and green kerosene lanterns for barge running lights. It was these very anachronisms that allowed me to play the best practical joke on Crash. It was a joke never spoken of until now.

One night Crash had one empty barge to bring to St. Paul from the Upper Harbor in Minneapolis. It was shut-out fog, but he decided to go anyway. He made Bernie and I ride the head with a walkie-talkie. Well we couldn't see anything either. When he ran under a bridge, we would make out the green and red lights of the navigation span through holes in the mist as we got close.

As we would pass beneath the green light we could see the bridge deck and hear the traffic overhead. Obviously he was moving pretty slowly. The chill in the air was very wet, the bone chilling kind. How to keep warm then? Eureka! I realized we could start a fire with the kerosene in the lamps. They each held enough to spare, and for some reason there was an abundance of scrap pieces of barge line lying around.

So we piled it all up and doused it with kerosene. I lit a match and said "Bernie prepare to get warm." It took a few tries to get the kerosene to catch in the damp air, but soon we had a nice fire smoldering. It smoldered well because the lines are made of woven recycled plastic. We couldn't stand close enough to the thick black smoke to keep warm.

Soon Crash was squawking over the radio, "Hey what's going on out there. Can you guys smell smoke? There must be a building on fire somewhere. Can you tell which side of the river it's on?"

"Ah shit!" The smoke was rolling along the top of the barge covers and straight back to the pilothouse. "Rats, shit, rats!" We started looking around for something to throw over the fire.

"Uh no Crash, we can't smell anything. I don't smell anything. Bernie do you smell anything?" I kept the microphone keyed on the radio so he could hear us both.

"Nope. I don't smell anything."

He must have got hold of the marine operator, because after a few minutes we could hear sirens of fire trucks and police cars from all directions in northeast Minneapolis. Then we could see searchlight and flashlight beams slowly crawling around through the fog on both sides of the river.

Out of the fog the green light of the Broadway Avenue Bridge navigation span drifted overhead. The fire diminished, leaving a molten pool of multi-colored plastic turning gray as it ran and mixed together on the deck.

"I hope it's cooled off before we get in the Upper Lock."

Crash's voice came over the radio again, "I sure hope they find that fire."

"Yeah me too." I touched the cooling plastic with the toe of my boot.

Lucky for us no one noticed the 10-foot circle of melted plastic on the deck, while it sat in the fleets awaiting a tow the next few days.

Don't Shoot the Messenger

"Those bridge tenders have a rough life, don't they Rookie?" Senator stretched back onto the smooth corner of a fiberglass barge cover. He clasped his hands behind his head for a simple pillow. We were floating dead in the water a few hundred feet south of the Savage railroad bridge. For their part, the two bridge men were toiling away at their big T-handle.

The T-handle is long enough at the crosspiece for a man to get on either end. The vertical piece is about as long as a man's leg. At the bottom end is a key for unlocking the short sections of rail that connect the bridge deck with the land rails. The two men go from one end of the bridge to the other and walk the T around in a circle to disconnect the rails. That done, they turn to the center of the bridge to operate a small electric motor that spins the huge bull gear on which the bridge span rests. Slowly the span turns until it's parallel to the river and the barges can pass.

The bridge deck is high enough from the river for the local towboats and barges to clear, except for the support girders. These act as joists for the deck and hang down four feet below the typical pilothouse. The girders stand perpendicular to the deck and are spaced about 15 feet apart. Most harbor pilothouses will fit snugly between the girders.

Most of the time, the bridge span is left open to river navigation. For many years there were periods during the season when local switch trains would need to use the bridge a week or two at a time. On each and every trip, our towboats traveling to and from the grain elevators in Savage had to wait for the bridge tenders to go through this 15-minute process. A boat working the few elevators above the bridge might need to make six to 12 round trips a watch. Waiting for the bridge can eat up a lot of time.

Experienced pilots would simply steer the barge so that they could squeeze the pilothouse right between the girders. It isn't terribly difficult, but if the steer isn't timed perfectly, if the current is in a crossing stage, or the tow slides even a bit, the upper decks and their inhabitants will be scraped off into the river like gum from a shoe. This can be costly and embarrassing.

Savage Bridge — note the low-hanging girders under the bridge deck.

Tending the bridge is hot work. To a deckhand building a tow down in the fleets, this little bit of grunt work seems laughable or like a nice break, but these are railroad employees raised on the public teat. So these guys had no patience with Crash, who was so scared of his own wake that he never considered "running the girders." So Senator and I would lounge atop the covers of our lone empty barge until the bridge was completely open, then we would signal back to the pilothouse.

"Comin' ahead," he'd announce over the PA horn. "All clear," as if he were driving 15 barges through a flood crest in St. Louis Harbor between the slippery piers of the Eads Bridge.

Traditional river roles had been drummed into me. It was not my place to speak up or speak back to Crash. He was the captain, and his word was law — regardless of how ignorant. Still, there were occasions when I witnessed others less tolerant of his status voice their opinions. These I was free to enjoy.

The best time was when I was chosen to be the messenger of one such opinion. I relished my role while enjoying a perverse immunity. The Savage Bridge tenders had no restrictions on their method of addressing Crash and his behaviors.

"You, hey you kid," the man standing on the railroad bridge turntable yelled down to me, as the barge I was standing on slid by him. I looked up and pointed to my own self and mouthed "who me?"

"Yeah you. You go back to that boat, and you tell that pilot he's the biggest chicken-shit pussy on the river."

The look on my face questioned what I might have heard.

"That's right. He's the biggest chicken-shit prick out here. He's the only pilot who needs this damn bridge swung open every single time he goes through. And you tell him I said so!"

"Okey-dokey," I cheerfully affirmed.

All the way back to the boat I whistled and strutted.

"Hey Deckster, what was that tender saying out there? Was it about the night opening schedule?"

"Not exactly." I could barely contain my glee.

"Well Dummy, what did he say?"

"He said you were the biggest pussy he'd ever seen. No wait, he said, you were the biggest CHICKEN-shit prick pussy he'd ever seen!"

It took a huge amount of will-power not to smile when I was done. I continued to stare at him.

At first his jaw dropped, and then his lips pursed together so tight I could hear them squeak. Spittle formed in the corners of his mouth as he began to grind his teeth harder and harder. Clearly he was weighing his options. I had uttered the words, but this was one time he couldn't ethically blame the messenger. After all, he had to assume I might never have uttered these profanities disparaging his character and skill if he hadn't prompted me.

He actually looked like one of those cartoon characters who gets so angry that steam whistles out of his ears and the hat on top of his head rises up into the air. "He said what?"

I took my time, to make it seem that it was hard for me to utter such an insult at my captain again. In fact, I wanted to relish each syllable like a fine wine as it spilled over my lips once more. He seemed to realize this as his face turned redder and redder by the second. I hunched my shoulders just a little and kind of shifted my weight from one foot to the other.

"He said…" Crash's face contorted visibly. "He said, (ahem) he said 'You are the biggest chicken-shit prick PUSSY he has ever seen.'" In my head I prayed "Oh please ask me to say it yet again."

It was beautiful. His face was scarlet. He was on the verge of a major grand-mal stroke. I waited for the volcano to blow. This would register on the Richter scale somewhere.

He looked death at me again, and then he closed the window and sat down on the pilothouse chair out of my view. Disappointed that the show was over, I sulked into the galley. We were already clear of the bridge, and the opportunity for fireworks was past.

Hours later we faced up to another empty barge to run up and spot at the elevator. When Crash rounded the bend below the bridge, I was standing on the bow end looking over the brown water as it slipped beneath the rake. The old familiar musty smell of the Minnesota River wafted up at me. The bridge span was already open.

Instead of continuing on up through the navigation span, Crash put the barge into an abrupt steer to the port. The barge slid on up the mud bar below the railroad tracks and came to a stop 50 feet from the little bridge-tender shack.

The two men peeked out the door. This was new to all of us.

Suddenly Crash came walking fast out onto the line deck of the bow where I was standing. He was apoplectic. Spit flew from his mouth as he started in cussing and challenging the tender who had been talking to me. They sat in the shack and just laughed at Crash. Crash looked over the end of the barge at the soft muck of the bank. It was a 13-foot drop, and he would have sunk up to his hips easily. Even in this state of mind he realized that he might make himself look even more foolish. His arms dropped to slap his thighs, his chin sunk to his chest, and he spun to head back to the boat. Utterly defeated, he had no other recourse. I came within a hair of feeling sorry for him, but I quickly dismissed that notion.

Senator came around from the other side of the barge at the same time. "What's going on here? I can't find Crash on the boat? He's not up there is he?"

"No, he came out and yelled a little, but he went back to the boat already."

He just shook his head and muttered something about working with dopes. When I looked back up to the shack, the bridge guys were shaking their heads too.

A Night in the Barrel

Aclap of thunder like demonic cymbals clashed just as I opened the
door to the battered Ford pickup truck. I looked in at the faces of
the two men sitting inside. A huge wet curl of dyed black hair hung down
over Crash's snarling lip. He reached up and pushed it back into place,
and looked at me like I was a bug. A wave of resentment pushed me
back.

"Well whaddaya waitin' for?" snapped Senator. "Get in while we're
only soaked!"

I clambered in and sat on the passenger side, up tight against Crash's
right side. Crash stiffened as I bumped up against him. I chanced a glance
his way and saw that his jaw was flexing and getting tenser than a fore
and aft wire. A few rivulets of rain ran from his thick hair down his cheek
into his evil looking mustache. His dark eyes glowered straight ahead,
burning a hole in the windshield. A shiver ran down my spine.

Senator guided the crew truck out of the parking lot under the High
Bridge along Shepard Road and over the I-35E Bridge. We could see the
boat and a couple of empty barges going under the bridge. Senator exited
onto Highway 13 and took a left towards the Pool and Yacht Club Res-
taurant. He stopped on the side of Lilydale Road, and we watched as the
Harry R. Harris day crew let the two barges loose to float upriver alone.
The red and white towboat turned around and headed towards us. As the
boat's steel hull scraped up against the rocky bank, we could hear thunder
in the distance.

We scurried down the bank and over the splashboard. Crash went upstairs to relieve the day pilot, and we crowded into the small galley to change with the deck crew. Senator and I engaged in a sort of dance with the other crew as they packed and we unpacked our gear. While we danced, we exchanged a few minutes of small talk mixed lightly with tow business. It is the kind of dialogue that takes place on any towboat at crew change. It is freewheeling and bounces all over the place.

"Where we takin' those barges?"

"Two empties for Minneapolis, like regular."

"Hey, who ate my lunch meat?"

"What are your night orders? Where will you guys be for crew change tomorrow?"

"Probably up around Savage. You get a day off from Minneapolis."

"Oh good. It's supposed to rain all weekend. Be nice to get some ridin' time."

"Yup, looks like we'll spend the night in the rain running the locks before we head up in the morning. Love those lock showers."

"Maybe we'll do it at the houseboat in the morning then. You'll never make a round trip to Minneapolis and get up to Savage by morning. How many we taking up there?"

"Yeah, I guess you're right. We're supposed to dig four out of the lower fleets when we get back down."

"Good luck. That's where we got these two, and North Star fleet is a jam-packed mess."

"Look, ya better keep an eye on the port main. It's burning a gallon a watch now."

"Did that center engine overheat again today?"

"Is the coupling tight? Are the tools out there?"

"Nope brought 'em back. There's a good line on the head. The one at the coupling is a piece of shit though. If you break the tow to tie off, you'll need a couple more good ones out there."

"Didja hear we're working through the weekend. No time off for the shift change again. Somebody might have to pull a 24 to make the switch."

"Well screw me man! Can't they get any trip hands? I ain't had a whole two days off inna month. I need to be drunk pretty soon!"

"I heard that."

"Shit!"

"See you in the morning. Try to stay dry!" More thunder crashes sounded in the distance.

The steps outside the galley thumped as the day pilot made his way down to get off the boat. He stuck his head in the galley and signaled "let's go" to his deck crew. All three scrambled over the splashguard, up the rocks and mud to the truck. Crash backed away from the bank and headed across the river to face up to a couple of free-floating barges.

Once he was faced back up to the barges, Crash put the hammers down on all three mains. Senator and I scrambled back down the tow-knees to the galley to settle in and plan our cleanup and maintenance chores. I was digging through my duffle while Senator finished putting his food away. From deep inside his bag he pulled a large jar full of nasty looking flesh.

"Okay Junior, you can have some of the pig knuckles, heh, heh, and for lunch I've got some home-made pea soup, made it myself. But keep your mitts off of my Kool-Aid, it's all I have to drink today."

Outside, the sound of thunder rolled and then crashed as the rain began to let loose. I closed the window over the galley table. Senator and I crowded the galley door and watched while the sound of the rain on all that steel increased. The drops were huge. When one hit the deck it splashed knee high. Senator sipped at his watery looking Kool-Aid.

We watched awhile as the rain ran down the slope of the head deck to pool up against the threshold of the galley door. Usually I liked a nice rain on the boat. Rain has a fresh smell that masks the aroma of diesel exhaust and rotting grain on the barges. But this was a lot more than a little rain. At our feet, the rain water mixed with the hydraulic oil under the winches to make little rainbows.

"Hey Senator," I said. "I was reading where on those old sailing ships they would use oil dripping from bags to calm the waves around the boat. Weird, huh?"

Senator took a swig of his Kool-Aid from a plastic tumbler. "Well it's going to take more than a little oil to keep Captain Crunch up there calm in this shit!"

We just stood side by side a bit longer, watching the beginnings of an adventure land on the deck in front of us.

"Well Junior, ya better head up and check on the high captain. He'll be getting antsy with this shit comin' down. He didn't sleep a wink today. As soon as it started raining this morning, he started worrying about the river rising and those empties in the wind up there around those narrow bridges. Dumb bastard never recovered from hittin' Hennepin Avenue. I'll be up in a minute. I gotta check the engine room."

So I made my own way through the engine room and past the steering pumps to the aft door. To my dismay, it was raining just as hard back there. I hunkered down and dashed for the steps leading to the second deck, dodged between the exhaust stacks and flew up the pilothouse stairs.

Once inside the pilothouse, Crash greeted me: "Gawddammit kid, you're foggin up my damn windows." He reached up to adjust the cheap defroster that was supposed to keep his front window clear. I watched Crash play with his cigarettes until he had three going at once. He juggled them from one ash tray to another and his lips. Occasionally he'd try sticking two in his mouth at once, and he'd rearrange them and start over.

This went on until we heard Senator stomping up the metal stairs. He swung the door open and pivoted inside quickly.

"Boy it's like a cow pissin' on a flat rock out there."

"Ya know what Draine-O says at a time like this. He says it's a real frog strangler!"

The three of us huddled in *Harry's* tiny eight-foot-by-eight-foot wheelhouse somewhat sheltered from the weather. The wind pushed rain through the small leaks in the windows and whistled and pulled at the doors. In just a few hours enough rain had fallen to justify adding a chapter to the Bible. The marine radio crackled with reports of breakaways in the lower fleets. Jets of water shot from the overflow pipes along the river between St. Paul and Minneapolis.

Through it all Crash steered two empty barges tied end to end towards Lock 1. Empty barges are like big sails 200 feet long and 18 feet high.

The wind banged against the huge steel sails. It was a challenge for Crash to hold them steady between the banks of the river. At times he had to point into the tempest and crawl upriver sideways.

When we cleared Fort Snelling I went below to put my rain gear on. Senator quipped as I got up to leave the pilothouse, "Looks like it'll be lock showers all night Rookie. Sure glad I'm the senior man."

This was a poke at me as the junior crew member. The deckhand with the most experience is in charge of the engine room and doesn't have to walk to the far end of the tow to signal into the lock chambers and tie lines to the wall.

The heavy raindrops crashed on my hood in loud thumps. The extra bulk of rain gear and my life jacket turned my walk into a slow shuffle. The hood cut my vision like blinders, and I had to feel my way along the slippery deck. When I reached the bow end I could saunter around freely, since there were no covers to snag my sleeve and jerk me off the side of the tow. Standing on the front end of the barge, I looked out into the rain and at the light steam on the surface of the water ahead.

The river was full of stuff washed off the streets of Minneapolis through the storm drains. Clumps of brown foam, wads of asphalt, bloated squirrel carcasses, baseballs, tennis balls, plastic bottles and condoms floated under my feet as we knifed through the brown water. Sticks and dead fish also dotted the surface of the river. The Mississippi might be wild and untamed, but she wasn't pristine anymore.

The tow continued to crawl up around Monkey Rudder Bend until I could make out the yellow and white lights of the Ford Lock and Dam. The lower gates were open for us, and the boat traffic light went from red to flashing yellow and then green. With my left hand straight overhead, I signaled Crash straight ahead. The barge bumped into the long land wall and rubbed into the cement. When the first barge went past the bullnose I waved "all-clear" with my right hand. The steel beast crept into the green-slime-covered chamber.

It was time for Crash to stop the engines and float, so I turned to face the boat and waved both arms horizontally back and forth like a baseball umpire signaling "safe."

"All stop," echoed in the chamber from the loudspeaker on top of the pilothouse. When the first barge was within 50 feet of the blunt end of the chamber, I faced the boat with both arms overhead like I was signaling a touchdown. I dropped both arms straight down in a "settle down" motion. The cavernous chamber echoed again, "All baaack!" The tow came to a gentle halt and nudged up to the cement beneath the upriver gates.

I looked up into the night and saw the shadow of a lockman on top of the wall. Silver streaks of rain drops were all around him in the light from the lock and the boat floodlights. "Whap!" his handy line hit the deck beside me. He hauled it back up after I knotted it into the eye of my lock line. He dropped the eye over a timberhead atop the wall, and I wrapped my loose end onto the kevel on the barge.

I stood there looking stupid in the rain. As the barges slowly rose through the big concrete box, I pulled slack out of my line until I was looking eye-to-eye with another sap too foolish to get out of the rain.

"Good evening Joe."

"Hiya Bob. Whaddaya say tonight? Some rain, huh?"

"Is that what it is? My old man used to call it liquid sunshine."

"Ha, ha. Where's he tonight?"

Someplace dry I suspect."

"Smart guy, your old man."

"Smarter than the two of us, doncha think?"

"Aww, I quit thinking an hour ago, when my brain got soaked. What the hell took you guys so long to get here?"

"Well look over that dam yonder and see all the current from this here flash flood."

"Hmmm, yeah. Well when did Crash call?"

"Down around Fort Snelling."

"Really?"

"Yeah. He likes to call early, in case if someone else above calls and get his lockage."

"Dumb bastard. You fools are the only ones out on a night like this."

"No, there's plenty of action down in the harbor. We're just the only ones up here tonight."

"Stay dry," he said ducking into his little shed on the upper end of the chamber. He twiddled with some knobs, and red lights went green and slowly the big gates groaned open. A whistle blared, Crash answered from the boat, and I collected my rope from Joe the lock tender.

We shoved out of the Lock 1 chamber and on up and through Lake Street, I-94, Washington Avenue and Lower St. Anthony as it rained harder and harder. Weather reports later stated that something in the neighborhood of 10 inches fell in a six-hour period.

The distance between the Lower and Upper Lock chambers is only about a thousand feet. As soon as a pilot steers out of the Lower Lock chamber, he is steering into the cave-like entrance to the Upper Lock. Crammed into the space between the locks is a General Mills loading dock, and right next to that is a sand dock — probably the same dock where J.J. Hill used to hump bags of flour before he got smart and made a barge-load of money.

Nowadays the site is dominated by the new Guthrie Theater. The new I-35W Bridge frames the landscape, and the short stretch between the St. Anthony Locks is an archeological park, where folks can come and see evidence of the city's history as the grain capital of the world. That night it was just a dark, crowded, nasty place to maneuver barges.

One of our empty barges needed to be placed at the General Mills dock, and Crash decided he would drag that load off of the dock by tying it to the side of his empty barges.

It sounds simple to throw a rope around a barge and just move it 200 feet to one of three tie-off cells. Each of the cells was round and about 20 feet across. Their steel walls were filled with concrete and encircled with eight-inch-thick treated timbers to cushion the blow when loaded barges bumped into them. Tows use them while they wait for traffic coming out of the lock. But, with the permission of the lockmaster, we'd use them to make the switches at the General Mills dock.

Over the PA Crash bellowed, "Just catch me some lines across to the load, and I'll drop it down onto the govermit cells until we come back down with the other load!"

Senator and I looked at each other through the rain. You didn't have to be a genius to know that was a stupid thing to try even under ideal conditions. A load is 10 times heavier than two empties, and Crash would have a hell of a time maneuvering the tow with a loaded barge tied to the side of two empties even if he wasn't near blind with the two deckhands crawling around in the dark and rain in between the load and empties. It is dangerous jumping back and forth and up and down decks that vary 10 feet in height when they are wet and slippery. It would take all of our skill and care to keep from getting hurt. How could we be his eyes and give signals at the same time?

The safe way would be to take the extra time to tie the empties up high along the old Sheilly gravel dock. Knock the boat out and move the load by itself. It would take several extra minutes, but it's a sure deal and makes a world of difference in safety.

We did our best in that weather. Senator was giving hand signals, while I was trying to loop rope around fittings on the load below in the dark. We took several false starts, but managed to get some sloppy leads from the empties to the load. After the load was loose from the dock, it took mere minutes for Crash to become totally unhinged with frustration. Each time he got the load moving back, it took several seconds for the lines to take up enough slack so he could work ahead to keep it from dropping too far or too fast. We only needed to move back the length of a barge, but we broke many lines before we were even close.

"What the hell! I can't see you. What? Come ahead now???"

Crack! Snap!

"All Stop! What? You mean to tell me both lines are broken? Sheeit! Catch me a line before that load slips by us and hits the lock."

"We got another line on it already you idiot!" Senator would scream in vain at the dark pilothouse. He had both wet-gloved hands clasped over our heads, but the searchlight was diffused in the heavy rain. All we could see of Crash were the raindrops slanting through the twin searchlights on either side of the pilothouse. He could hear nothing we yelled from 400 feet ahead of him.

Eventually we convinced Crash to knock out and move the load down by itself after we tied the empties off to the wall of the dock.

He groused about it when we came back to the boat, but Senator simply told him it had to be done the long way — that it would take less time under these circumstances. He still didn't believe it, but we got stubborn with the rain running down our faces.

We needed only to tie the load off, break our empty loose, head up, drop it off and light boat back down here for the load to St. Paul.

An hour or so later we were northbound with one remaining empty, headed for Packer Terminal at the head of navigation on the Mississippi. Our southbound load was tied to the cells above the Lower Lock. The empty for General Mills to load tomorrow was hanging on the wall, ready for us to push in and finish tying when we were light boat on the way back.

I was below in the cramped galley when the Lower Lock called Crash on the radio. "Lower Lock to the *Harry R. Harris.*"

Crash answered, "Yes, *Harry* back on channel 14."

"Hey, *Harry Harris*, something is wrong with that load you guys tied off on the cells. It's broke loose and looks like it might float over the dam!"

He clued me into this conversation shortly after I headed to the wheelhouse in response to his leaning on the call buzzer. For the next half hour he fretted and chain smoked and chewed me out non-stop.

"Gawddamyoo Deckster, if that load goes over the dam it's your ass. How many times do you have to be shown how to tie lines! Your damn line must have come loose, the lead slipped off and that damn load is loose. You have got me in a world of trouble, ya stupid sunnavabitch punk kid. Gawddammit… gawddammit to hell anyway!"

This litany continued through the landing procedure, his tinny voice seeking me out in the rain and lightning over the PA system. All the while Senator and I were scrambling around tying lines in the rain.

Senator was no better. In two years, it was the only time he'd ever taken Crash's side against me.

Those two rode me as much as we were riding the boat, noisy and droning. I was starting to wonder what havoc I might have caused. At first I'd been sure that my knot, though leading up from the barge at a steep angle, had enough hold to stay on, even in this slippery rain. Still, doubt began to creep in. I spent that short ride back down to the Upper Lock hunkered down like a convicted felon.

The image of a loaded barge crashing into the lock and dam, tearing up the thick cement walls, killing the helpless lockmen and being flushed over the top of the dam, sent a cold shiver down my spine.

"What have I done?" I wondered.

In the lock chamber I tended my line from the galley door. On the galley table was my paperback. I stepped over to pick it up and went right back to leaning against the open door jamb. I tried to read a few pages from *Moby Dick*, while the boat groaned at the lock line. All I could manage to do was watch the floating lock timberhead bob up and down in the recess slot. The rain slipped down the mossy green cement chamber wall. I wondered how all this compared to one of Melville's "Nantucket sleigh rides." Crash would have got on well with Ahab. For sure he was ready to knock my hat off.

As the massive gates began to open, Crash had the searchlights on, aiming the beams through their widening crack. The pouring raindrops shown like bright diamonds as they crossed the beam of light. My heart was jammed right up in my throat by then.

The *Harry* slid through the calm waters inside the rock jetty that enclosed the distance between the locks in this little harbor. The searchlight swept back and forth over the rough waters beyond, where the rapids flowed under the old Stone Arch Bridge. We could not see down to the dam yet.

Suddenly there it was. The load was cross ways in the river, pointed for the dam, but it wasn't moving. It was poised to go, but still next to the cells.

Suddenly, as quickly as the rain stopped, the terrible voice of God in the wheelhouse went silent as the boat touched up to the lower end of the swung-out barge and gently began to nudge her back. Senator and I stepped over the splash board onto the gunwale and walked down to the lower end and around to the inside.

"Aww shit!" It started to rain again.

Quickly I scurried up to the bow to see if my rope was broken. On the way past the quarter kevel on the stern I spied the line Senator had tied, floating in the rain-dimpled river all curly cued, the eye still around the kevel. My line was still on and holding, though bone tight, being pinched against the cell with the other end pried away. Looking through the darkness between the cells up near the bank, I saw the culprit: A six-foot-wide storm drain was shooting out a stream of water at least 70 feet long to a point where the side of the barge had set. It had pushed hard enough on the 1,500-ton scow to cause Senator's line to slip through its knot and come loose.

"Look! That's your line came loose, not mine!"

"Hey Junior, that's your rope, not mine!"

There and then it hit me like a clap of thunder. Senator was completely pickled. He had no idea where he'd been when we tied this barge off. He'd always been strict about the protocol: The green guy ties off the head and the utility man takes care of the stern, nearest the boat, in case something should go awry with the engines.

Through the torrent of rain, a flash of lightning illuminated his face and the line hanging off of the side of the barge. It was floating in the water, serpentine like a big tired water snake.

A few minutes later, after both men had gotten extremely quiet, we headed over to the dock to finish tying off the empty. It was raining every bit as hard again. I had to jump down onto the dock to tie off the stern. The dock was set along a curved wall on the river, and since we had tied the head off in a different spot than usual, the darn empty wouldn't come in and lay flat on the wall.

The huge grass lines the dock workers used were absolutely soaked, and I was not strong enough to throw the wet manila line 10 feet in the air and out another 10. I tried a few times in the dark, and started to walk back to where Senator had been on the bow. By now Crash was quite frustrated and had stopped shoving the barge over. When I got up there he had the boat against the wall itself beyond the barge.

"Why in the hell don't you have this thing tied off yet?"

I blew up. "Because, you stupid bastard, you never got it in close enough to the wall to where I could get a line!"

Well that did it. Ever since he and Senator had realized they'd been yelling and riding an innocent man, Crash needed an outlet. Finally I had done wrong, so his anger at me was justified.

He came down from the pilothouse and slogged in his cowboy boots through the mud puddles of the dock, down to where the line lay in a foot of water. He picked it up and made a loop with the bight and threw for all he was worth. His throw also fell short with a splash.

In the dim light from the dock lights, he stood facing me. His pearl-buttoned cowboy shirt was untucked and drooped wet over his tooled leather belt. His hands were clenched in tight fists waist high at his sides. He was shaking with blind rage.

I took a step back into a different puddle. A flash of lightning lent his face an aspect of evil. The shadows around his eyes were sinister. It crossed my mind that he could kill me with his bare hands, and there would be no witnesses. He could simply dump my limp body over the edge of the dock into the river. The extra current from the flash flood would sweep me over the dam and destroy any forensic evidence pointing to murder. I took a few steps backwards because he was ready to snap, and with his strength I didn't want to be within arm's reach.

We stared at each other through the rain for a couple of minutes. I was shaking from fear and cold. He was still shaking, and his chest was heaving. I watched closely to see if he was calming down, and his breathing seemed to slow down, but I kept my distance to be sure.

Finally Senator walked down the side of the barge, and Crash threw him one end of the rope. Senator pulled up some slack, and after laying the bight around a fitting threw the end back at Crash. He tried to catch it, but it hit him on the head and knocked his cowboy hat into the puddle.

He bent to pick up the muddy hat, while I finished tying the rope off. We slogged back to the boat with him several steps ahead of me. Crash wearily climbed up into the pilothouse and pulled the PA microphone to his mouth. He took a deep breath before speaking.

"Listen here you smart ass, if you ever talk to me like that again I'll fire your ass!"

I grabbed my duffel off of the galley table and scurried to the top of the port towknee.

"Hey you prick! I quit. Take me over to that lock wall and let me off!"

He raced over to the long riverside wall of the upper lock and got the towknee within a foot of it then backed hard. I swung my leg out ready to hop off, and he reared hard on the engines again to pull away from the wall.

"There! You're lucky I don't fire you!"

As the boat pulled away from the wall I yelled, "What are you talking about. Get back over there you prick! I quit. Get me off of here!"

He ignored me. "Yup. Damn lucky."

Anger I could understand, but what happened over the course of the next couple of hours blew me away. It became clear in my mind, like an illumination of lightning, that I was dealing with a form of insanity. Crash was still trying to blame someone else, and it had to be me. That was the order of things. But I was innocent, and in his subconscious he knew that to be true. Still, I had to be the one to blame and in order to do that he had to enlist the help of Senator.

I sat in the galley pouting after we departed the Lower St. Anthony Lock chamber. After awhile the buzzer rang. "To hell with him," I thought. "Let that old fart Senator answer him. They deserve each other."

The buzzer rang again. Crash had a way of ringing the call buzzer that was amazingly demonstrative. I knew he was getting impatient.

I shuffled out onto the head deck and stood without looking up. I knew he was looking down waiting for me to appear in my place.

"Get Senator, I need to talk to him. I need to talk to someone who can understand a simple plan."

If he wasn't in the pilothouse and he wasn't in the galley, he could only be in the engine room or steering room. Sure enough he was passed out on a pile of life jackets on the floor of the steering room in the stern. His snoring was louder than all three main engines, the turbochargers and the whine of the hydraulics powering the rudders.

I kicked at his feet. "Get up the high captain requests your presence above."

He grumbled and looked up at me. "What the hell does he want."

"How should I know? He buzzed for you."

"Godammit, I can't leave you dumb bastards alone for a minute!"

Minutes later the call buzzer rang again. "Get your ass up here!"

Once I was in the door of the pilothouse Crash spoke to me. "We talked it over, and we're not going to tell Draine-O what you did. He'd fire you for sure fer nearly losin' a barge next to a dam."

It didn't even occur to me to act surprised or get angry. I had found myself in the middle of an ugly triangle. The only reason Crash kept me was because he needed a whipping boy. He had to have Senator, because no one else would lead him around the harbor by the hand.

For his part, Senator worked with Crash because Crash ignored or didn't notice his drinking. They couldn't afford to lose me, because I had put up with their shit where few other experienced deckhands would. Above all, they were keeping me from advancing to the pilothouse myself.

It was becoming clear to me that I needed to get away from this fool of a pilot before someone got hurt. And it seemed Crash was determined to keep me under his thumb and not allow me to escape his grip. The only way I would ever get any steering time that mattered was to work with some other pilots.

When Captain Brown tormented Sam Clemens, he dreamt of killing him a thousand different ways. I was there with Crash, but I had neither the nerve or, more importantly, a plausible opportunity. Sam belted Brown when he'd reached his saturation point, but I hadn't the nerve for that either. Besides Crash was built like a gorilla, and Senator said it would "take a two-by-four across the back of his head to get his attention, and then he'd just be pissed."

Any chance to work with another pilot I got, I took. I figured that sooner or later I'd get a chance to jump ship, if I kept my eyes open.

Pencil Whippings and
Brown Water Mutinies

"Damn Dexter, that sumbich is pencil whippin' us over here."

"What is pencil whip?"

"You know what it means. The damn fool runs aground at Lower Lyndale [a difficult bend in the Minnesota River], and instead of logging that time he puts extra time on the tow work we did in the fleet digging and rigging the barges. We get charged with his lost time."

"Oh I see."

And that is what Crash would do. Any time wasted steering badly or running aground or just taking too long to deliver a barge, he wrote in the log as time spent in the fleets waiting for his crew to complete their part of the job.

Crash never learned from his mistakes and was absolutely stupefied when Jimmy and another deckhand rebelled in the face of his abuse. They were working at rigging a raft of barges one afternoon for the Cargill line boat *Arrowhead* to turn south with.

Jimmy and the green deckhand were trying to "square-up" the tow. It is a way to get two barges lying side by side to be flush on the ends, using wires tightened in the opposite directions. The first wire has to be laid while the boat moves the outside barge up and down. Jimmy would lay the wire around the fittings on each barge and then hook it. Once the ratchet is hooked to hold the wire fast, Crash would backup or push into the wire lead.

It can take a few attempts, depending on how close the mate wants the ends to line up. On the last attempt Crash backed into the wire before Jimmy had the ratchet fastened. The wire instantly took a strain and came tight. Before he could slide the keeper ring over the pelican hook, it forced his grip apart. The pelican hook snapped out of his hand and squashed the fingers on his right hand pretty good. Luckily nothing was broken, but he had to stand there and rub his hands for a few seconds.

When Crash saw him standing around he began to rail at the two deckhands for not working fast enough. Jimmy tied a rope to hold the two barges together and walked back to the boat to give Crash a piece of his mind while he allowed the feeling back into his hand.

"Hey we're doing the best we can. Things would go a lot faster if you concentrated on holding the barges still instead of screaming at us."

"Don't you tell me how to handle a boat," he thundered back. "You just get out there and lay those wires right and quit screwing me up!"

Well, Jimmy went back onto the tow all right, and he gathered that other deckhand with him. Then they walked to the bank side of the barges and shinnied hand over hand on a tight shore wire until they were standing on the sandy bank by the St. Paul Airport.

Soon Crash was on the loudspeaker, "Jimmy turn on your walkie-talkie, I can't see you out there."

Jimmy answered on the marine radio channel 18. "We're over here by the anchor piling. Going to walk up there to the road and hitchhike back to the office."

"You get your asses back here to the boat right now!"

"Nope, not going to do it."

"I am the captain, and I'm telling you to get your ass back here."

"Well I am a free man, and I tell you that I'm quitting. You can just set there on your boat and suck hind tit for all I care!"

The reality of the thing set in on Crash hard. "Please Jimmy. Please come back. How am I going to knock the boat out? I'm stuck here."

"That's your problem. I'm tired of your shit, and I'm tired of your yelling, and I am tired of bein' pencil whipped by your dumb ass."

"Aww c'mon. I won't yell anymore."

"Apologize."

"What?"

"You heard me. Apologize." Before they clambered back onto the barges, Jimmy made Crash plead hearts and flowers over the radio while they giggled. The rest of the harbor boats switched over to channel 18, and every swinging dick in the harbor heard Crash eat crow.

After Jimmy jumped boat on him, I never heard Crash apologize to a deckhand again. Sometimes he reacted to his embarrassment by increasing his abuse. Ironically, he expected that abuse to be returned as loyalty. I don't know how many times he assumed we would back up his lies to the boss. He instructed my partner Harry to lie for him one night.

It was our job to stand on the covers of high empty barges and direct him with hand signals. We would stand in the glare of the searchlights on opposite corners and peer into the dark ahead. In very narrow places, like slips with barges on either side, this can be tricky.

He banged into the corner of another barge in one of the South St. Paul fleets one night, because he didn't steer away when Harry signaled him.

"Hey. Any damage to the barges?" he asked weakly over the loudspeaker. On our hands and knees with flashlights, we inspected the steel corners as best we could.

"Yes," I signaled by waving my flashlight vertically at the pilothouse.

An hour later we were tied off at the wharf barge back in Pigs Eye Lake Fleet waiting for the owner of the fleet to show up and see what we'd done. I was at the sink doing the dishes and cleaning, while Harry sat at the galley table cleaning his kerosene running lanterns and trimming the wicks. Crash wandered through the galley trying his various excuses out loud, fishing about to see which ones we might accept.

"That damn barge was half tore loose and swung out at us, didn't it boys?"

We kind of looked at each other.

"Boy was that wind howling all of sudden. Why it came outta nowhere and slapped me against that fleet."

We looked at each other and then at him. The silence was deafening, and he got that we weren't buying it. He slunk out of the galley and into the break room on the wharf.

"That man is out of his mind if he thinks I'm going to tell a lie for him!" Harry shook his head.

Finally our boss and the shipyard manager showed up at the wharf. We ferried the assemblage over to the damaged barge. Harry and I stood on the head deck while Crash pulled away from the wharf in Pigs Eye Lake. We could hear the conversation in the pilothouse as clear as a bell. Mostly it was Crash making excuses.

"I tell ya Draine-O, if those two could have given decent signals it never woulda happened. And then the wind picked up and blew the damn barge out in front of me!"

Harry looked at me and shook his head. In a few minutes Crash pulled up alongside the empty barge and held the boat next to the corner in question.

The two men looked it up and down from the head deck. They could inspect the entire corner easily. The manager traced his finger over the crack. There was some hurried whispering, and then Draine-O stepped back and looked up at the pilothouse.

"Crash ya gawddam fool, this here is old damage. Look at the rust! This thing was already scheduled to have this little crack welded up. Take me back to the wharf, and please don't ever wake me up because you're scared of the dark again!"

Crash began to ride Harry harder, heaping on the verbal abuse. He didn't know Harry like I knew Harry — there was a limit to what Harry would take.

Harry Christian Baxter was from Lake City, Mississippi. A retired Marine Corps major, Harry had done a tour of duty in Vietnam. He was a friend of my father and wanted to try his hand at river work. In my 19-year-old eyes he was a hero. Six feet tall with chiseled features softened by his green eyes and quick smile, Harry spoke with a polished drawl. He would stand in the door of the galley looking out over the river and roll his cigar back and forth as we talked.

But to Crash, Harry was the new guy and so was going to be the one to pick on. He yelled at him, talked down to him and always put me on the spot. "Show him how to do that Deckster!" Harry's resentment over this was growing by the day.

Finally after a particularly trying afternoon digging two empties out of Airport Fleet to take to ADM, Harry had reached his saturation point. This fleet was a notorious time eater. It was shallow, and the shore wires were so long the tiers of barges swung around a lot and got in the way of the boat and the targeted barges.

We all had a tough time of it, and Crash vented his frustration on Harry the entire time, mostly over the PA system. Harry grumbled under his breath as we untied and retied lines, and picked up and transfered shore wires to get our barges cleared up.

When we were all done and finally departing the fleet, Harry and I resumed our stations on the head deck. He stood in the galley door chewing thoughtfully on his cigar, and I faced him seated on the center bitts. We were, each of us, in the cooling-down mode when Crash, leaning out the open window above us, made some off color remark about how things would have gone a lot smoother save for Harry's ineptitude. This was patently uncalled for, as the flavor of any chore has everything to do with the pilots planning and very little to do with the deckhands carrying out his wishes in the fleet.

Harry threw down his cigar and said "That's it! Me and Crash are going to have a little talk!" Well I knew they'd already had several talks, and Harry had the look of a man ready to talk with his fists. Crash deserved it, to be sure, but I didn't want Harry to get in any trouble. I positioned myself in the doorway and said "Listen Harry this is not the way to settle this."

Placing his hands in my chest he gave me a little shove, and I flew up and onto my back. He reached out to pick me up saying, "I'm sorry Robert, but I've had about all ah'm going to take from that piss ant."

I stayed down on the head deck — not wanting to be in the middle of anything between two such large combatants — and cocked my ears to hear what I couldn't witness. I knew it would be a bloodbath. Crash was strong, but my old man once saw Harry knock a guy across a barroom with one punch while seated on a barstool.

Harry came down a while later absolutely red in the face. "That bas-

Crestfallen, Crash slipped down to the Smith Avenue High Bridge. There Crash backed in, and we tied the barges off temporarily. Light boating back up to the bridge Crash had us in full blown rescue ranger mode. "Get the bumpers out and tie them along the port side. See if we got any full cans of gasoline, blah, blah, blah."

Senator listened to all this and was just shaking his head. Finally when Crash was finished, he looked up and said "Okay Crash, and I'll boil some water too, in case they have a baby."

A barge sits close to a lock wall.

As we closed on the houseboat a ways above Omaha Bridge, the light from our floods illuminated several older men in suits surrounded by young women in miniskirts and tight, low-cut blouses. For sure it was a business cruise. We sidled up to the boat and caught a couple lines on the port side of *Harry*. From the pilothouse Crash directed the operation as though we were towing the *Queen Mary*.

"Get the slack out of that line. Okay I'll back on that one, and then you get the slack out of the towing lead." And on it went until he very nearly floated down into one of the bridge ice piers. Senator just shook his head again.

Later, after we'd delivered them safely to the small boat docks at Harriet Island, we light boated down towards Pigs Eye Lake for our northbound barges. The three of us sat in the pilothouse in the dark. Crash was beside himself with glee.

"Didja see all them women? Hooooee, they were gooorgeous! Hooooeee, I wish we coulda stayed there! Didja see that cute redhead? She was lookin' at me, and boy she had a big ol' smile and some real nice breasts!"

Finally Senator could take it no longer. "So Crash you like those girls huh? Which one do ya want?"

"What do you mean, 'Which one do I want?'"

"They're hookers, you dimwit. Half of 'em work at Allery's downtown. I can fix you up with that redhead."

At that Crash turned around with a look of utter disbelief. In the moonlight through the windows we could see the dumbest look cross his face. "NOOO! You don't say! You mean them girls is prostitutes. I don't believe it. Wellllll I be gawd dammed! Wow, hookers, I be damned! Wow!"

The Setup

Some days later we nearly ran over someone we couldn't help. The three of us were sitting together again driving the old Ford pickup back from crew change up in Savage. The truck swayed as we went from one curve to another along Warner Road headed for the wharf barge under the High Bridge.

The heads of Crash and Senator shifted from side to side as they napped. It was always fun to jerk the wheel back and forth to get their heads bumping together.

"Bang" they'd awaken slightly and grumble at me to watch out and then nod off again. I could always blame the curves, bad road conditions and traffic of Shepard Road for sloppy steering.

At the time Shepard Road ran straight down to the river from Randolph. It curved between the old NSP Power Plant and the new one. Capitol's wharf barge was across the street from the new plant and right underneath the old High Bridge. The parking lot and entrance from Warner was a tight quick right turn. It was a dangerous little maneuver, and we witnessed many accidents there over the years. Early one winter a young woman in a Volkswagen Beetle did a barrel roll right over the barrier and landed right side up in front of a group of us. She was unhurt but seriously shaken. We calmed her down and sent her on her way. Not so lucky were the folks who took the long way down from the bridge.

When I reached the break in the cement road barriers, I turned quick to avoid being rear ended and then slammed on the brakes extremely hard.

Both of my delicate passengers banged their heads on the dashboard.

"Hey dumass, what are ya trying to prove!" Senator snapped at me.

"Dexter, you punk, I'm going to kick your ass for this!" Crash growled.

"What the hell are you trying to do kill us?"

They looked over at me, rubbing their foreheads and necks. I pointed across the steering wheel. Lying on the asphalt under the front bumper was a sprawled inert body. At first I thought maybe one of the other deckhands had seen us coming and was playing a joke, laying down in the road ahead of us. But then I saw that the legs were pointed in impossible directions and there was a lot of blood on the asphalt around his head.

High Bridge

"Oh great!" screeched Crash.

"Now you've done it. You've gone and killed someone!" added Senator.

"No, I didn't. He was laying there when I pulled in."

The guy had landed in our parking lot under the High Bridge.

"Damn fool missed the river altogether," Senator quipped.

"Holy Jeezus it's a jumper!" said Crash.

Sure enough some poor slob had exited the High Bridge, voluntarily, or not, and missed the river completely, on purpose, or not. We never found out if it was foul play, or not.

But the way Crash handled the police, when they arrived, gave me a wicked idea. Crash had been all over the boys in blue to get his name right and to make sure they recorded that he was the high captain of the *Harry R. Harris.*

While I watched him work the policeman taking notes, I had an inspiration. "I'll spell your name right," I thought. While he was busy bullshitting the cops I hastily scribbled a note in my best girlie-style handwriting:

Dear Crash,

I have a huge crush on you. I was on the houseboat you rescued the other night. I was the one with the red hair.

I am trying to work up the nerve to talk to you in person.

Ever since that night you rescued us I have dreamt of standing next to you in the pilothouse of your mighty towboat.

Love,
Your Secret Admirer

It was as corny as I could make it, even down to dotting the "i" in admirer with a little heart. I slipped the note under his windshield, walked down to the wharf barge and punched out for the night. The note completely slipped my mind.

The Sting

Several days later Crash showed up for work in disguise. We heard him walk down the metal steps to the houseboat. He stuck his head in the door and mumbled, "Let's go." His cap was pulled low, his cowboy shirt was buttoned up tight around his neck, and he sported the largest pair of sunglasses I've ever seen on a man. He wouldn't talk to anyone, and he hustled us out to the parking lot. We left quickly to find the night crew.

Hours later Senator and I made our way up to the pilothouse to see Crash. Without his cap and sunglasses, we could see that he had a black eye and scratches all across his face.

Later on, when just the three of us sat in the galley, Senator cornered him, "Okay Crash, what's the deal? What truck ran over you?"

He turned meekly to face us. I shuddered at the severity of his wounds. It had to have been a close encounter with a badger or some other vicious beast.

"Awww hell, it was the wife. She found this note in my pocket when she was doin' the laundry. It was from that hooker last week. She wants to go out on a date with me. The wife flew off the handle when she found it. Why in the hell didn't I throw it away?"

With that he took off his shirt. When we saw his back and chest Senator and I gasped. He was covered with scratch marks and bruises and what we later learned were rug burns from when she dragged him unconscious to the basement steps and rolled him down. She locked him in the basement overnight.

After we had gone below, I told Senator my part in the affair. He sat for a long while at the galley table looking out the window as the river bank passed by. Finally he stood up and walked over to me. He put his hand on my shoulder, and his thoughtful look transformed into a huge smile. For the first and only time in two years he looked at me with respect.

"Kid you made my day. You just made me the happiest man alive for today. The guys at Awada's are going to be real proud of you for this."

Crash's Cold Shoulder

It was beginning to sink in that decking for Crash was no easy path to the pilothouse. He would make me steer when he needed to leave the bridge for something, but he refused to let me steer any of the tricky spots or to teach me anything about navigating the St. Paul harbor.

This fact landed in my head with a thud during the last days of the 1978 towing season, when we got banished from Minneapolis. We were banished by the lock master at St. Anthony Falls when Crash scared the hell out of all of us.

It was beginning to look like a cold winter. A shelf of ice had grown out a good two to three feet from the cement lock wall in the lock chamber. Each time the chamber filled, a little more froze along the wall at the top. This narrowed the chamber by about five feet when it was full. The chambers of the St. Anthony Falls locks are 55 feet wide. This accommodates a 35-foot-wide barge and set alongside it the typical harbor boat, which is 19 feet wide.

With the chamber narrowed by the ridge of ice, there wasn't enough room for the boat next to the barges. We found this out on the way upstream. At the bottom of the chamber, where ice did not form, the chamber was as wide as always and the boat set over easily. After tying the *Harry* to the side of the tow, I went back onto the barge to tend my lock line.

We rose quickly in the chamber as we normally would. Near the top of the chamber Jan Janos, the older brother of future Minnesota Governor Jesse Ventura, leaned over the wall to say hello. When he opened his mouth, however, I could hear only the sound of screaming over the PA mixed with the blare of the air horns. Jan and I looked back to the boat in time to see Crash ready to leap over the side. Hurrying to the side of the barge where the *Harry* was tied off, I saw that the starboard side of the boat was hung up under the ice and in danger of sinking as the water continued to rise in the chamber.

Lightning fast, Jan leapt to his control shack and shut the fill valves. Then he opened the empty valves until the *Harry* settled down level. It took an hour to knock enough ice off the wall to get *Harry* and the barges up high enough to depart the lock northbound.

From the lock all the way up to the docks in north Minneapolis I was busy chopping ice that had formed on the side of the boat and around the rudder controls on the stern.

The lock master was hopping mad when Crash came back southbound with two loads instead of one. With just one barge the boat can stay faced up, and the lock is plenty wide for one 35-foot-wide load by itself.

"Is he insane?!" he asked me as Crash scraped down the side of the chamber with the lead load.

"He's got a plan, he thinks," I answered.

I was using hand signals on the bow to guide Crash close enough to the wall to try and scrape off the thickest ice. It didn't work all that well, and when he set *Harry* over it was hard on the wall and the side of the boat.

"That's it! You guys are done up here! I am calling the Corps, and these locks are done for the season."

In those boom days, barge companies pushed tows in and out of St. Paul until the river froze over. The first season I worked for Crash, the harbor was open until December 3. And the next season, we sent the last tow out of town from Red Rock Fleet in South St. Paul four days before Christmas.

We built the last four loads out of Savage as the snow began to fall lightly along the Minnesota River. By the time Crash steered through the navigation span of the old Cedar Avenue Swing Bridge it had turned into a full blown blizzard.

The loads Senator and I were on eased forward glacially. The rigging was buried under a drift of snow that reached as high as the fiberglass covers. It took several minutes to clear enough snow to find the ratchets and wires.

The deckhands from the line boat stood shivering in their brand new insulated coveralls and felt-lined boots. My hands were stiff and ached from the cold. My leather work gloves had never dried completely from handling wet lines earlier in the day. For several hours they lay across the top of one of the main engines and had dried stiff, but the first line that got wet in the river soaked them through as we tied off one of our loads. Now my fingers were screaming in pain.

One of the other deckhands was ready to go home on days and now he was forced to work over when his relief missed a flight into Minneapolis.

"Gawd damn!" he yelled. "People ask me what I do for a livin', and I tell them I work on steel. I sleep on steel. I live on steel. I work with steel! Nuthin' but steel. I'm turning into friggin' steel!"

As I hung up the face wires I glanced up at Crash in the pilothouse. A flurry of thoughts raced through my half-frozen mind: "The box looks warm. He's wearing just a shirt and no gloves, and he's got hot coffee and cigarettes. I need to get into the pilothouse. I got a license. I bet I could handle a boat."

I headed up the stairs at the back end of the *Harry* leading to the second deck and on to the pilothouse. Through the window I could see the old fart pouring a fresh cup of coffee. Steam rose like a cloud out of the cup. My own breath crystallized in front of me.

Inside the pilothouse I sat behind Crash on the low red-cushioned lazy bench. Removing my frozen gloves was a huge chore with numb, stiff fingers. They hurt, they ached, and when at last they were free the real pain set in. I clamped them under my armpits and fought back tears.

Crash spun around and glared at me. "Look what you've done to my windows. They're all steamed up! Git your ass outta here."

So I went downstairs and found a spot between the piles of drying ropes and lock lines spread out on the deck between the engines to warm up.

"I have got to get away from this bozo."

Northbound into Ignominy

All of Crash's meanness came back to haunt him towards the end. His nerves unraveled as the deckhands began to treat him as a dose of bad luck, a modern day Jonah. Working for Crash came to mean extra work, verbal abuse and the opportunity to be blamed for one of his foul ups.

The tragedy of Crash was that he was a guy who wanted nothing more than to be a river pilot, but in the end it was the thing that drove him crazy. The Mississippi will take your strengths and weaknesses and magnify them. Your weaknesses and flaws will haunt you to the last. The thing that makes real stories different from fiction is redemption. In a made-up story the tragic figure comes to a crisis, and his character development leads him to or away from redemption.

Harry needed no redemption, because he was one of my war heroes. He had offered the ultimate sacrifice willingly. Senator, the old grouch, suffered a massive head injury when a broken hook slammed into his forehead at light speed. The subsequent change in his personality made him unrecognizable to me, but he died a hero. As a volunteer fireman for Newport, he and his crew answered a five-alarm fire in Stillwater at one of the waterfront warehouses. The roof caved in while he and two other men were on top of it, and he fell into the burning basement. His dying screams were heard by a survivor, who claimed they were the most horrible sounds he had ever heard.

Crash never got his redemption. If he ever had a chance at redemption, he turned his back on it. Instead he continued to alienate and berate his crew mates. His paranoia had hardened his soul so completely that the light of redemption never could get a foot in the door.

Over and over again he naively expected that people would reward his behavior by going to bat for him. In the end, his doctor gave Crash some pills for his nerves. They calmed him down but made him even more dangerous. He just seemed to be in a fog most of the time. I sat in the pilothouse with him as he abruptly turned his one barge around in front of a downbound line boat with 12 loads.

On his last watch he tore up a crane barge under a low bridge and tried to blame the miscalculation on the deckhands. He claimed that they weren't watching carefully enough, when in fact they were screaming bloody murder at him that the boom was not going to clear. He couldn't hear them over the sound of some jag-off country singer whining about a flat tire on his pickup truck and his loss of innocence, on KDUH-AM radio. In the end Crash self-destructed, and that was the last straw for the boss. He canned Crash for lying. Crash slunk back to his hometown, and I never heard from him again.

Final Grade in a Crash Course

L ater, after I earned my own piloting position, I carried with me one important lesson from my experience with Crash: how NOT to run a boat. One night on a fast-rising creek full of driftwood, I guided the *Mike Harris* down the Minnesota River with six loaded barges. The current ran swift and strong as the old boat negotiated the "S" curves by the Minneapolis Airport.

Totally focused on the swing of the 650-foot-long raft ahead of me, I barely noticed the mate slip into the dark pilothouse.

Next to my left shoulder I heard Jimmy say, "Howz it goin' deckster?"

"Hey Jimmy. Not too bad I guess. She's sliding all over the river tonight."

"Yeah, I see. Say, are ya having any trouble with your steering?"

"No, why? Should I be?" and I looked at him.

"Well it's just that you got a whole frigging tree sticking out the ass end of the boat is all, so I was — you know — just wonderin' if the rudders were hanging up at all."

"No way" and I turned to look out the back window. I couldn't see anything, because the rear windows were blocked by the exhaust stack housing. So I turned on the side flood lights and squeezed past Jimmy to the door.

Sure enough, there was 30 feet of cottonwood jutting out and up from under the propeller-and-rudder end of the boat. It was odd because the amount of wood stuck underneath should have been rumbling and breaking off rudders and snapping propeller shafts.

"Where did that come from?"

"I don't know. I was down in the engine room, and I stepped out onto the stern for a smoke and just about walked into it."

"I better try to get it out of there before it snaps a shaft or tears off a rudder then," I said as I silently recalled the incident from a few years before involving Crash, the two empties and the joke Senator played on me.

"How are you going to do that?"

By then we were entering a short, straight stretch of river above the Mendota Bridge. When the tow was pointed straight, I backed hard on all three engines and braced myself for anything. There was great rumbling and clanging under the hull, and the tree rotated a whole quarter turn. The branches vibrated and shook. Then the thing stopped as if lodged in tight.

The 30 seconds or so it took to do this pointed the tow at the bank, and we needed to come full ahead quickly to keep from crashing and sending six barges loose down the river headed for the bridges of St. Paul. With the rudders hard down, the tow slowly straightened up. The rumbling had stopped, but the tree was still there. The steering and propellers all seemed to work just fine, so I returned to the task of navigating. "Well I guess we're going to go downriver with our own personal tree."

"Looks that way," Jimmy said.

I thought about how Crash would be having a major stroke about now, and I decided to ignore the tree. Twenty minutes later we were coming around the bend at Lilydale looking for the Omaha Railroad Bridge. This can be a tricky affair in high water with cross currents and nasty bridge piers, so I was watching my stern and saw that that tree had come out all by itself somewhere.

"Good thing Crash ain't out here tonight," Jimmy said from the lazy bench behind me. "Be just his luck to run over that damn thing and sink something after you dropped it!"

Paddlefoot, Crackerjack Pilot

Mark Twain had a name for especially skillful pilots: he referred to them as "crackerjack lightning pilots." He included the skilled, the uncanny and the lucky pilots in this category. During those years from 1975 to 1980 I had the good fortune to work for one of the luckiest pilots on the river.

In 1974 Draine-O had hired a young man off of some local excursion boats to train as a towboat pilot. The rest of the towboat crews decided he should have a nickname that reflected his roots on the hot-dog boats, so they called him "Paddlefoot." Decking for Paddlefoot was always exciting. He had been born with excellent piloting instincts.

I learned that his good luck was born of his laid back attitude. That's not to say that he didn't take his piloting seriously, but where Crash worried his way into trouble, Paddlefoot trusted that whatever trouble he got into he could escape by his wit, talent and good fortune.

A warm, pleasant summer day on the Minnesota River found Senator and me sitting in the galley of the *Mike Harris*. We were just sitting down to lunch when all hell broke loose and the general alarm began to ring like a major disaster. The alarm was followed by the deafening blast — over and over — of the powerful Kahlenberg air horns signaling impending doom.

Only minutes before the *Mike Harris* was peacefully pushing a raft of steel grain barges that weighed about 5,000 tons and was 450 feet long by 105 feet wide. The rig was being artfully guided by our pilot, Paddlefoot.

He was entering a series of tight "S" turns on the Minnesota River near Pike Island. The approach to each of these turns is blind. It is not a place where vessels should meet.

While Paddlefoot steered down the narrow, twisting Minnesota River, Senator was busy in the galley preparing a meal of his famous pot roast. I took Paddlefoot his supper plate and stood there a few moments, while he situated his plate on the console. I watched as he passed under Airport Bridge. "Bridge" is sort of a misnomer, because Airport Bridge is a rack of strobe lights for one of the runways at the Minneapolis airport.

"Bon appétit," I said as I left to go back down the stairs to eat my dinner. Senator was already eating when I sat down at the other end of the small galley table. Only a couple mouthfuls into the job we heard the alarm bell and then the set of four brass horns blow several short urgent blasts.

"Damn pleasure boats," Senator muttered between bites.

The horns sounded again, only this time it was a prolonged blast. Out the window we could see the legs of Airport Bridge.

"Must be some yahoo driving too close to the tow," said Senator. He wiped his mouth and turned to look out the front window.

The horns blew a third time. This time four short blasts were followed by some scratchy cussing over the loudspeaker. Four is the official Western Rivers Coast Guard danger signal.

Paddlefoot was screaming over the loudspeaker now. "You better get that damn boat out of the way! That's right where I'm going to be in about two minutes."

I dashed out the door onto the head deck. "What's up Skipper?"

He leaned out the open pilothouse window directly above me and yelled down, "Oh there's some guys anchored under the power line fishing right in the middle of the damn channel!"

Jumping over the splash guard onto the barge, I climbed right up the short ladder to the barge covers. Senator followed right behind and scooted around the outside barge gunwale on the port side.

I could see the fishing boat ahead of the barges. An 18-footer with two guys in leather jackets fishing off the stern. Sprawled out on the bow, sunning themselves, were two shapely blondes in bikinis. Well they weren't

600 feet away and centered right on the jack staff.

Paddlefoot yelled again for them to move. All four heads turned in our direction momentarily and then back to their immediate business.

"That's it. I'm going to have to put her to the hill!" he said angrily. I moved to walk out to the head of the tow, but the pilot stopped me. "Stay here Bobby, be safe and wait 'til the rigging finishes raining down from the sky."

From where I was standing I watched in absolute awe as the bow end of the tow swung wildly towards the bank on our right.

Senator on the port side could see nothing of this, save for a lot more river on his side than there should be. "What's going on? Is he going to run aground or what?"

It was a moment before I could speak, but then I was able to blurt "He's already aground. He's got one barge halfway up the bank, and its knocking trees over like toothpicks!"

"Cut it out Junior I asked if he was going to hit the bank."

"I'm not joking. That starboard lead barge is up out of the water mowing down trees on the mud levee."

"Really?" He clambered up the covers to stand next to me. "Shit that's a real steamboat-in-a-cornfield moment!"

When the people in the small boat saw what was happening, one of the fisherman pulled up their anchor and they motored slowly off down the river. Incredibly, the four loads slid gently off the mud bank and back into the Minnesota River without losing any speed at all, and we continued down the river like nobody's business.

When I finally looked back at the pilothouse, the pilot was already sitting down with his feet propped up on the console. I could only shake my head and wonder "What's next?"

Paddlefoot took a quick glance back at the row of downed trees and shook his head too.

Senator watched the small boat disappear around the bend at Mendota Bridge. "Well I hope we didn't put 'em out none."

Towboat pilots learn a whole book full of rules to avoid collisions on the river. They work their way up to the pilothouse after years on deck, steer for an accomplished master, then take a battery of tests and sign off on a Coast Guard license that states they are competent to handle tons of steel in a narrow and shifting channel.

All that a pleasure boater needs to sign is a bill of sale. We were about to get lesson-one on why this is a bad idea. Hopefully an amateur boater learns some lesson from his narrow escape, his close call.

A half hour later, when we had recovered somewhat from our close encounter with dry land, the pilot was coming around the bend under the bluffs where Shepard Road intersects with Otto Street. It is a blind approach to a very tricky bridge. The cross currents at Omaha Railroad Bridge, in Lilydale, are nasty. Once the tow is coming around the bend the pilot had better be lined up just right on his marks or 5,000 tons of grain and steel will interface with concrete piers.

What happened next defies logic. Those clowns went a few miles downriver and anchored in the middle of this narrow navigation span of the bridge. When the pilot saw this he restarted his screaming over the loudspeaker and pulled on the horn so hard and so long that the air-compressor in the engine room kicked in.

After a few seconds that seemed an eternity one of the fishermen stood and switched places with one of the bathing beauties in the front of the small boat. Casually he hauled the anchor line up and set it down in the bow. They putt-putted out of the channel slowly. It helped that the bridge tender went out onto the tracks and gave them a short education — seasoned with four-letter words — on the rules of the road regarding right-of-way situations.

Paddlefoot was the son of a minister and as such lived up to the tradition of straying far afield of his father's footsteps. He was no saint, but I was beginning to think that if this man can drive barges over land, he just might be able to walk on water.

Sleep Towing

Twain told a story about a sleep-walking pilot. This pilot came to the wheelhouse in the dead of night, while sound asleep, and steered a dangerous bend, to the astonishment of witnesses.

Modern day harbor pilots work 12-to-14-hour stretches, seven days a week, often for weeks on end. Fatigue plays a big part in the way much of the work is done. Everyone up here has heard the stories about pilots dozing off at the sticks. It is almost unavoidable. Senator and I witnessed one such time that — only by a miracle — did not end in major disaster.

Senator and I were in the stern storage room washing the bulkheads. It was repetitive dipping the rag into hot soapy water with a cup of diesel fuel mixed in and wiping engine soot from the once glossy white walls.

When it was time for a break, we stepped out onto the stern for a smoke. The boat was passing under the High Bridge around two in the morning. We stood there admiring the scene unfolding behind the boat as she made her way downstream through the St. Paul waterfront — the High Bridge with the full moon poised overhead, the marina on the west side, the Farmers Union Elevator and the Cathedral on the downtown side as we were nosing under Wabasha Street.

We weren't talking. We were just standing on the ass end of the boat enjoying the view, when the engines abruptly slowed down and the wheel wash behind us became calm. I looked over to the starboard side of the boat and saw the Wabasha Bridge pier just 50 feet off the stern and straight abreast.

This is not the time to be stopping the engines, because the Robert Street Bridge was a scant 400 feet below us. That's when I glanced forward up the side of the boat and saw that the tow was pointed for the wrong side of the navigation span.

Senator was aware at the same time, because we looked at each other and took off up the side of the boat. Quickly Senator ducked into the galley and handed me a life jacket as we headed out to the head of the tow. Behind us we could hear Paddlefoot cussing himself. The PA was on, and he was barely audible, talking to himself. "What a time to fall asleep. Damn it. Downbound through the bridges in St. Paul!"

By now the engines had been full astern for almost a minute, and we could hear the 48-inch propellers starting to dig into the water.

Senator and I were in the fast walk mode, and reached the head of the tow in 30 seconds. He went to the port corner, and I stepped to the starboard. We'd each reached our respective corners when the tow was only 50 feet or so from the ice piers of Robert Street. These piers are only 69 feet apart, and our tow was 70 feet wide. Never mind there wasn't enough clearance for the pilothouse 400 feet behind us. We each signaled him to the opposite side, because there was no room either way.

Fortunately for all of us, Paddlefoot awoke soon enough to slow things down considerably, for when we struck the bridge the outside corners slowly ground to a halt inside the tapered piers and stopped, then a small chunk of cement fell onto each corner of the tow at our feet. Paddlefoot continued to back up on the barges and soon had the tow straight in the channel and headed under Robert Street. No one was ever the wiser.

This was getting spooky. This pilot seemed to be untouchable. Certainly he was level-headed and unflappable. Perhaps he really could walk on water.

Hanging by a Thread

The old adage about your life flashing before your eyes before you die is — in my experience — a load of crap. The night it happened to me my one big thought — the only thing on my mind — was "Oh shit! I gotta get outta here! Now!"

One thing about decking on the mighty Mississippi River: You don't need a lot of barges, high winds, towboats and a lot of other river rats to have a high old adventure. A person can scare the shit out of themselves all alone on a calm, peaceful night.

I was alone the night I damn near killed myself. My night shift aboard a harbor boat in St. Paul had started out peacefully. We were just knocking around downtown St. Paul. All we needed to do was make a couple trips up and down through the harbor removing loaded barges and putting empty ones in for loading the next day.

Under a full moon the diesel towboat *Mike Harris* slid gently past Lambert's Landing at St. Paul's riverfront. The lights of the Robert Street Bridge and the surrounding buildings reflected in the Mississippi River. Ribbons of white, yellow, red, blue and green trailed away from the barge we were pushing. The end of my cigarette glowed red hot, and the smoke mixed with the fishy smell of the water. I was enjoying this quiet scene all alone, perched on a cold steel timberhead at the front end of the barge.

The only sound was the "whoosh" of the bow wave. Watching the simple effect of a box end shoving against the river always mesmerized me. The water climbs almost to the deck of the square at my feet before it falls off to the side. I flicked my cigarette into the water and peered at the dark shadows of the Great Lakes Coal Dock, trying to see the empty barge we would be picking up alongside of this loaded barge.

The light of the radio tower atop Dayton's Bluff swung its red beam around overhead. We neared the wall, and I could begin to make out the outline of an empty barge. "This must be the one Paddlefoot aims to grab," I whispered to no one. The only other person working the deck with me was back by the boat getting ready to catch a line at the stern.

Paddlefoot backed hard on all three engines, and the sounds of diesel turbos whined. Moments later water splashing against the stern end of the barge added to the cacophony. Squinting into the glare of the flood-lights on top of the boat, I could see Frisby winding up getting ready to throw his line. The line uncoiled as it went up and over the fittings on the empty — a perfect throw, which he quickly bent over to tie in the dark.

The current flattened the load against the other barge. I heaved my line up into the darkness. The bight landed over my head with a light thud. I pulled hard to make sure it was around something solid. A small shower of coal chunks landed on and around me. "Got it." I bent down and tied the end of my line around the timberheads at my feet.

Frisby and I scrambled up the covers on the load and pulled ourselves up onto the deck of the empty barge at the same time. We walked in-board, and he turned the upriver end loose while I turned the downriver end loose. I stepped into the glare of the searchlight and raised both my arms in surrender. "All gone!" I shouted at the boat.

"All gone then," Paddlefoot answered over the PA system. We could hear him announce his departure on the marine radio and the roar of en-gines. Paddlefoot put one astern and one ahead to twist the tow back into the river.

"*Mike Harris* to Pigs Eye Bridge. We're working away from the coal dock and heading your way. Can we get an opening?"

"Roger Cappy. There's no trains for awhile, so I'll have the bridge open for you."

I sat down on the highest corner of the empty away from the pilot-house, in case Paddlefoot needed some hand signals to get by the bridge pier he wouldn't be able to see behind the empty.

"That's okay Bobby. I can see good enough with just these two."

I waved back at him and sat awhile anyway, it was such a nice night and all.

Fifteen minutes later the bow wave washed up against the bridge pier, and I was bored with all the beauty. I climbed back down on the load. I felt around in the dark for the towing line. It was stretched pretty thin from the strain of dragging the empty. "I suppose I should double up this headline."

With my flashlight I picked out the extra line and prepared to throw it on. As I stepped into the throw my ankle rolled on something, and I threw myself right into the river. Going head first into the river I thought the last thing I would ever see was the moon overhead. With both arms flailing on the way over the side I had managed to grab the tight tow rope. The rushing water pulled me down to where I was immersed and bouncing in the wake.

Next thing I knew, I was looking up at the end of the empty barge about to run over me. "Musta slipped on something," was all I could think.

Somehow I held the end of the rope firmly in one hand. The wave from the barge was pushing against me. If I let go of the rope I'd be sucked under the barge and sucked through the four-foot-wide propellers of the boat. The water was cold, and the force of the barges moving forward was working against my grip.

From day one on deck I'd been told, "You fall in the water around the tow or the boat, and you're as good as dead!" There were tales of men bumping along underneath barges and miraculously surviving. But there was that deckhand awhile ago who'd disappeared on a night watch only to be found in pieces along the riverbank in the Pigs Eye Lake slip. They said he walked off the front end of a barge in the dark and got chopped up like bait in the propellers of the towboat.

"Better hurry, this water is cold!" With all the effort I could, I swung my left leg up. I hooked the edge of the deck with my foot. Pulling with both arms and one leg I broke free of the rushing grip of the river and hauled myself up and over the edge of the barge. I slumped onto the deck and lay on the cold steel for a minute. After that minute I stood breathing hard with relief at a very close call and surveyed my wet clothes in the dark. With my flashlight I cleared the deck around my feet and threw the double up line on and secured the two barges with the extra line.

"This is too nice of a night to get run over by a damn barge," I said walking back to the boat for dry clothes. Over on the bank of South St. Paul some kids were tending a big bonfire. The pilot swung the searchlight over and lit up their drinking party. They whistled and hooted, "Hey can we go for a boat ride too!?"

Illuminated on a muddy stage, they all moved a step closer to the bank to raise their beer cans in a unified salute. Together they hooted-n-hollered, "Whoo hoo!"

"Hey take us for a ride on the Love Booooat!"

I shook my head and focused on where I was walking. "What a buncha clueless boobs," I muttered to no one. The water gurgled in the open space between the two barges, and I looked down and thought about how close I had come to being squeezed down there. Up and over went the bight of the line.

"Oh yeah it's just a big old Love Boat ride out here!" I yelled back. This was answered with more hooting and a salute of beer cans. "That's the problem with people, they just don't have a clue what goes on out here!" I mumbled to myself.

Then a last voice from the shore party, the loudest one, "Hey Dude, we wanna go waterskiing!"

That old chestnut again. He had made a crack about how slow we were. Paddlefoot swung the searchlight around over my head. I raised one wet arm up over the shadow of the coaming I was standing behind. The light hit my arm. "Oh there you are. I was wonderin' what happened to you."

"Damn" I thought, "Getting into the wheelhouse is hard enough — all the shit I have to learn. Gotta live long enough to try though."

My job now was to walk into the galley like nothing had happened. Back in the galley Frisby spotted me changing into dry socks.

"What happened to you?"

"Ah I got my feet wet. Tripped and darn near fell in the river."

"You know the rule…"

"Yup."

View of the I-35W Lower Lyndale Bend on the Minnesota River from the pilothouse of the *Lois E.*

Close calls on deck seem to come when you least expect it. Long hours and fatigue cause you to drop your guard when the work slows down, and that's when bad things can happen.

Waterskiing

Paddlefoot never heard me that night, and if I had got run over, it would have been some time before anyone would have missed me. Steamboat Bill had filled me with stories of guys getting run over by a boat, and body parts found days later floating in the fleets. He had seen a guy fall between two empty barges and manage to catch himself on the edge of the deck. Before he could pull himself up or the other deckhands could get to him, the barges slammed together. When they were able to get him up, Bill said, it was a sight "I'll never forget. All the blood in his legs and chest was squeezed up into his head like a tube of toothpaste, and it got big as a basketball. He died awhile later. It was not pretty!"

That last season I decked for Crash there was a night that was so foggy that one of the boats pushing barges from St. Paul to Savage, on the Minnesota River, had to stop at the fleet below the mouth and wait for a break in the fog. In the wee hours of the morning, a breeze blowing downstream blew away the fog, and it was time to go. One deckhand went out alone to turn the barges loose. He was never seen alive again. It was unclear if he just walked off the head of the tow or slipped and went overboard. His body washed up downstream a few days later.

Even though it is a constant hazard, the deckhands take the risk casually. To worry about it would just slow a man down. Common sense is the best remedy for danger. But sometimes a little blind luck can play a huge role in one's fate.

Brian Brezinka was my first mate on the *Sophie Rose* one night in October 1993. The water was getting cold by then, but the air was pleasant enough. He and a first-year man named Adam were down on the head deck splicing broken lines while I steered up through downtown St. Paul. It looked to be an easy night, with just two empty barges bound for Savage. It was Saturday, and no other boats would be on the Minnesota. The stern of the boat cleared the Omaha Bridge as I made the last call for traffic I would need to make.

"*Sophie Rose* is northbound at the Omaha Bridge standing by for any traffic coming out of the river mouth."

I knew no one would answer.

"*Whippoorwill* downbound at Mendota Bridge with 15 loads."

"Drive 'er Cappy!"

"Remember what Murphy used to say, 'Don't fuck up.'"

I leaned forward to close the front window. Brian and his partner were done splicing and coiling the leaving lines on the head-deck.

Brian looked up at me. "We're done here Skip going to take a break now."

"Okey-dokey." I closed the window.

We cruised by the darkened Pool and Yacht Club and the *John Theodore D.* tied off to the flimsy floating dock beneath the terrace. Howard and his first mate Lois came onto the bow and gave a wave. I reached across the pilothouse and flipped on the overhead light and returned the wave.

Then I settled back into my chair with a cup of hot coffee and tuned the radio to a station playing some 60s rock-n-roll. With no possibility of meeting another vessel, I propped my feet up on the console between the throttles for some low-pressure driving.

Not two minutes later I began to hear things. Spooky things.

"Bbboooobbbbbyyyyyyyy."

Was I hearing things?

"Bbbbooobbbbbbyyyyyy."

The hair on the back of my neck stood up. Skeeter warned me about the nights on the river bringing out ghosts and spirits. I reached over and snapped off the radio.

"Bbbbooobbbbbyyyy."

"Am I losing my mind!? Surely I am hearing things."

I leaned out the starboard side door and looked down to see one of my deckhands hanging onto a face wire for dear life. His feet were skipping in the bow wave and he was screaming at the top of his lungs "Bbbbboooobbbbbyyyyy!"

The *Sophie Rose*

In one motion I leapt back to the console and pulled both engines to neutral. By the time I was back at the door to see how he was doing, Brian had jumped out from the engine room and pulled Adam aboard by his shirt. Thank goodness I had Brian on board, who had sense enough to be alarmed when the engines shift out of gear, or Adam wouldn't have lasted much longer.

When the two deckhands were safe, I went back inside the pilothouse and continued upriver past the I-35E Bridge. The incident left me a little shaken as I realized how close we had come to losing a man.

A minute later Brian stepped into the house and moved to the coffee pot.

"Bob, I don't know for sure what happened, but it seems old numb nuts was doing some unauthorized waterskiing."

He stood in the door dripping wet and shivering.

"Why are you up here?"

"I wanted to thank you. You saved my life."

"Thank Brian. He pulled your ass out of the river."

"I coulda drowned!"

Then I found myself repeating the words of Steamboat Bill from years before. "You'd have been lucky to drown. Those wheels would have chopped you into hamburger is more likely what woulda happened. Rule number-one on the river is 'ya don't fall in. If ya fall in, you're dead.' It's that simple. Brian get his wet ass down to the engine room and wrap a fire blanket around him."

Party Time

The Minnesota River Valley around Port Savage is a short walk from some dense suburban areas. Bloomington and several other areas surround our little nature reserve. Kegger parties were always springing up along the banks at night.

Paddlefoot was pushing an empty through the port one Saturday night in 1978 bound for the uppermost dock, Continental Grain. Turbo and I were behind him on the lazy bench of the old *Mike Harris*. We were shooting the shit in that cramped pilothouse — more than likely complaining about having to work while everyone else is out having fun.

We crawled by the Cargill docks and Paddlefoot steered the narrow "S" turn leading up to the Savage swing bridge. Since the water this night was low, he ran under the swing bridge. Carefully eyeballing the underside of the bridge deck, he judged he could just squeeze the pilothouse and the searchlights between the girders that hung down.

It was not unusual to see people standing on the Railroad Bridge waving as we went under. This night they were lined from one end to the other. We waved and hollered while Mike blew the four brass horns in celebration.

Then we slipped out of sight under the bridge. On the other side we turned to look out the back window. All three of us ended up in a tangled mess on the floor as broken glass and rocks rained down around us. Mike did a brilliant job of steering from beneath the console until we were out of range. The party goers had broken nearly every window on the boat.

We got up off the floor and brushed glass shards off of ourselves. Turbo and I went out to tie off the barge. As we knocked the boat loose, Paddlefoot was calling the police on both sides of the river in hopes of corralling the miscreants. A quick survey of the mess we had to clean up got us absolutely riled.

Turbo yelled up at Paddlefoot, "Hey set us off on the bank over on the point where they can't see us. I want to sneak up on those bastards!"

I grabbed a toothpick out of the port tow knee and whacked the center bitts with a shivering clang. "Yeah, I want to bust some heads just like these windows. Look at this mess, those rotten effing pricks!"

Paddlefoot dropped us off with a toothpick each and the walkie-talkie. So here we were, a couple of deckhands with three-foot-long steel bars, a radio and life jackets sneaking through the woods to find these punks, while he took the boat slowly down towards the bridge as a decoy.

There we were making our way down a dirt road in the dark headed into a nest of drunks bent on our revenge. We were two commandos, two rough hombres, two tough guys, two complete idiots.

Pretty soon we were hunkered down in a thicket of bushes trying to make out which direction the voices were coming from. It wasn't long before we realized that the party was much bigger than the dozen kids on the bridge. Indeed we were surrounded by a sizable mob.

Turbo spoke to Paddlefoot over the radio, "Where are those cops? I think we are in some trouble here."

"Well where are you guys anyway?" Mike squawked while Turbo tried desperately to muffle the radio.

"Not so loud. We're surrounded here."

By now we could see several small bonfires a couple hundred feet away and on all sides. Through the darkness we could make out many, many shadows flitting about. We got even lower in the now seemingly small clump of bushes. I looked over at Turbo. We were both fondling our toothpicks. "What are we going to do with these?" I whispered.

He shrugged his shoulders.

Before we could panic, the cavalry arrived. The trees came alive as strobe lights broke up the darkness. Police squad cars weaved their way through the woods and surrounded the party. In a matter of minutes the cops were checking I.D.s and taking stories as we stood up and sauntered through the crowd. One cop looked us up and down and shook his head. "What are you guys supposed to be?"

"We're off of the towboat. You don't need us for anything do you?"

"Nah, I don't think so."

"Good," and we were gone. Soon we were sliding down the bank and crawling over the splashboard onto the bow. "C'mon, let's get the hell away from here."

"Everything okay?"

"Yeah, yeah. Just go, now!"

It was awhile before Turbo and I felt cocky and tough again. For weeks every time I heard a clang I flinched. Whenever we passed under a bridge Turbo and I would sort of sidle under a nearby overhang and scan the bridge for activity.

It's Raining Men!

Rocks weren't the only things thrown from bridges around town. People also had a way of finding their way into the river from the top of a bridge. In the summer of 1978 the river along St. Paul seemed to be filling with bodies. People were jumping from the bridges in droves.

It started with the time Crash, Senator and I nearly ran over one in the parking lot beneath the High Bridge. The boss, Draine-O, and a deckhand named Steve had to launch a rowboat from the houseboat to rescue a woman jumper one afternoon.

A short time later, a guy just missed a load of gravel as a tow passed beneath the High Bridge. Admiral, a deckhand on the *JoeAlJim* that day, jumped from the head of the tow into the river and held the guy up. The pilot floated along while Admiral and his tow slipped past and were pulled aboard by the other deckhand from the stern.

Aboard the motor vessel *Harry R. Harris*, Draine-O was spotting empty barges down at the old Farmers Union One dock. Harry and I were his ace deckhands. As soon as we were knocked free of our barges we zipped up there to assist. By then paramedics were all over the place at Harriet Island. The Admiral cradled this kid onto our head deck when we touched up. Light boating over to the landing and the waiting ambulance, Harry and I stood on the deck looking at this poor sap. His arms and legs were broken, and a wad of snot had blown out his nose all over him. Barely conscious, he was trying to speak.

"What's he saying?" I asked Harry.

Harry, a grizzled old vet who'd seen combat in Vietnam, just leaned against the galley door and shrugged while ruminating on his cigar.

So I bent down, getting my ear closer and closer to his mouth until I could hear a wheezing whisper, "I wish I wouldn't of done that."

Harry shook his head. "Hindsight is always 20-20."

But I looked down at the poor bastard and felt bad for him.

A few days after that, I was sitting in the spacious pilothouse of the *Harry R. Harris* sipping bad coffee on the lazy bench. Paddlefoot was driving four loads between Wabasha Street and Robert Street.

I was half listening to his conversation with Old Melvin who was piloting the *Mike Harris* elsewhere in the harbor. When we had slipped quietly under Robert Street something over on Shepard Road caught my eye. The sun was setting behind us, so I thought it might be a trick of the light.

In the time it took me to turn my head a white object fluttered from the walkway of Robert Street onto the west-bound lane of Shepard.

"Oh my god! Did I just see a jumper?"

"What did you say?" Paddlefoot swiveled around in his chair.

Pointing back I said, "I think I just saw a guy jump into traffic on Shepard Road!"

"Hey Mel, the kid here thinks he saw a jumper from Robert Street."

"Aww, he's just jumpy from seeing all those bodies lately!"

I shut my mouth and slunk down in my seat. Minutes later I turned around to see several flashing lights from emergency vehicles. I reached forward and tugged gently on Paddlefoot's shirttail. When he twisted around ready to snap at me, I gestured back to the bridge. The number of emergency vehicle lights had doubled.

"Aww shit, you're right. Huh!"

Night of the Living Dead

Things on deck at night can get really weird when a guy is working half asleep. And when the whole crew is sleepwalking, then all bets are off.

Night shifts are hazardous for the whole crew. There is not much to be done about the wave of exhaustion that sweeps over a body somewhere between 2 and 4 in the morning. No amount of caffeine can overcome the body's natural urge to snooze at that time of night.

Working nights on the Mississippi River can have a deckhand stumbling around like a drunk. Twelve-hour shifts that run into 13- and even 14-hour stints can be very fatiguing. So after 10 straight nights of these shifts, One-Eyed John and I were ready to cut loose and blow off a little steam. We got off the boat that last morning and first headed for our separate pads in the same Highland Park neighborhood of St. Paul. Then at the crack of noon we headed straight for our favorite river-rat hangout in West St. Paul. It took all my focus to sit on a barstool, but Johnny was up and dancing. I had to rub my eyes in utter disbelief.

I never imagined that One-Eyed John was such an amazing dancer. But there he was, in the space between the bar and the dining tables drunk as a skunk yet still able to spin a young lady around. Somebody found the old jazz tune "In the Mood" on the jukebox. As soon as he heard it, John grabbed a young secretary from the table next to us and started doing some Charleston moves. He was on his toes pushing and pulling and arching and doing something called the Lindy Hop and was very light on his feet.

"Hey Twinkletoes go for it!" I whooped

John had a long history on the river. He worked at Minnesota Harbor Service, sometimes called the Circus, for a few years in the early 1970s and came back several years later when we worked together at Pilot River Transportation. John's dad had taught him to swing dance years ago, and with two sisters he got a lot of practice growing up. His proper name was John Taylor and he grew up in Hopkins, Minnesota, but the river rats knew him only as One-Eyed John.

"Hey John Taylor is back in town."

"Who?"

"John, the guy with the red hair."

"Oh you mean One-Eyed John, the guy who used to wear a monocle when he decked at the Circus."

"That's him."

So there we were exhausted after 10 straight night shifts and too stubborn to get some proper rest. Determined to have some fun at last, we were engaged in a progressive drinking expedition and had made our way to the first stop where we ran aground on a couple of barstools.

Willy, our crew dispatcher, told us to expect a week of sitting on the sidelines and thought it a good excuse for some "day drinking." Well, we were into it and didn't notice when the phone behind the bar rang. The bartender answered and spoke quietly for a few seconds. John and I were engaged in a spirited talk about procuring a sailboat and changing our lifestyles drastically, when he thrust the phone between us.

"It's for you."

"Who is it?" I asked taking it from him.

"I think it's Willy, he's looking for some deckhands."

"Damn!"

I had been thinking we were safe to pursue a day of fun, and now the crew dispatcher had caught up with us at this well known river-rat hangout. That season of 1985 was a slow one, because the Carter Grain Embargo finally caught up to the barge shipping on the Upper Mississippi. The season was so slow that I worked on deck between piloting gigs for my company, but I wasn't happy about the demotion and even unhappier about the prospect of being interrupted at play.

I cupped my free hand over the speaker end, "Great now what?" Into the phone I said, "Yeah who is it?" Of course it was Willy the Worm.

"It's me. I got some work for tonight. Who's with you?"

I put my hand over the phone again and John leaned in to whisper, "What's up?"

"It is Willy and he wants some deckhands tonight." John leaned back and pantomimed a big groan. Into the phone again I said, "Look Willy, I'm with John but we been drinking all afternoon. It's not safe."

He ignored my warning, "We got to fire up the *Katie Rose* tonight and you guys are going to be my deckhands."

"Really? So you think when you need to jerk us around we're just layin' on the couch waiting for you to call?"

"Of course!" he quipped.

I choked the barrel of the phone briefly with both hands. "Look Willy, seriously, I'm in no shape for a night shift. We just got done working nights this morning, and we haven't been to bed yet. You said we'd be off for a week or so. Can't you get anyone else?"

"Nope. See you at the wharf by six." And he hung up.

"What kind of dope would ask someone to work at night without a decent amount of sleep?" John spat.

"It's hard to take that from someone who never drove anything but a hot-dog boat. Did I tell you about when I went with him to get the *Itasca* off of the dry-dock?"

"No. Do tell." John signaled to the bartender for a couple more beers. "Oh and a couple cups of joe for a chaser."

"Good idea, that coffee. Yeah, so anyway, there he is. He's standing between the sticks. We're in the water, and the lines from the dock are loose. He looked like he was going to piss his pants, he was so nervous. Hands ashakin' and beads of sweat on his forehead. I said 'Hey Willy, all you gotta do is back straight up 50 feet and drive away!'"

John shook his head slowly and took a careful sip of coffee. "Humph, I'm convinced that the only qualifications to be a dispatcher is a genuine and burning desire to avoid real work." Then he hooked a swallow from his bottle.

"Drink up we gotta get going."

Two hours later we were standing with unsteady legs on the wharf barge in Pigs Eye Lake. The pilot we landed was in similar shape. This had all the potential of a real interesting night working with a crew of zombies.

We made short runs for several hours. *Katie* was a light-assed boat with skinny face wires. That meant she was easy for a sleepy pilot to handle, and the lifting wasn't likely to kill John or me. Clearly we were all in need of some serious shut-eye, because each of our performances deteriorated over those few hours.

When a deckhand slows down, it isn't too bad. If he can keep from falling over the side or getting crushed, he will get through a long watch. However, when a pilot gets drowsy the potential for disaster cascades. When a pilot nods off, or "micro sleeps," some real bad shit can happen.

After a few hours of work John had managed to jam his shoulder against a barge cover hard enough to leave a bruise, and I was stumbling around on a slight ankle sprain. The pilot, between yawns over the loud-speaker, had narrowly missed taking out corners on a couple of barges when John woke him up by yelling at him from the bow. But a miss by an inch is as good as a mile in the middle of the night.

Round about 3 in the morning we were headed from the ADM dock up around Mendota to the fleets of South St. Paul. That is the magic hour, when despite four pots of coffee the human brain wants desperately to shut down for some rest. It also means that the trip from ADM to the fleets in South St. Paul will afford the deckhands a half-hour nap. It also means the pilot is without a baby-sitter to keep him awake.

Before we took to our beds John took the pilot a fifth pot. Then we curled up on the galley floor for a 15- or 30-minute nap. It is surprising to learn how comfortable a life jacket can serve as a mattress when a body is bone tired. The engine and propeller vibrations are real soothing at that hour. It only took me a moment to lose consciousness on the floor.

I woke with a start. Something deep in my subconscious, some innate alarm clock, woke me in time to look out the starboard window and see the stockyard lights. Then the squeal of the rudder hydraulics hard down got loud enough to be heard over the main diesel engines.

I kicked at John's boots. "Hey shake it out. We're here."

"We can't be. We just laid down a second ago."

Bumping into each other in the darkened galley, we tried to get our life jackets on. We got tied up once briefly when somebody's arm went through the other guy's armhole.

John was walking the gunwales while I made my way across the steel covers. Walking the tops allowed me to see most everything around the boat and tow. I must have been more than a little woozy, because I didn't see that we were about to run head on into a tow of 15 loaded barges.

If I had been awake, I would have signaled him to abort, but it took all my focus to walk across the ridges and valleys of those covers without breaking my neck in the dark.

John, walking down on the side gunwales of the barge, yawned and said, "Are we close?"

"Getting close." I stopped to look ahead. The pilot had his searchlights on by then, and there was some shadow ahead I strained to make out. Then with some urgency, "Holy shit he's going to ram the fleet!"

I began to yell at John to head back, and I started to sprint back waving my flashlight to alert the pilot. Casually one searchlight came on and then the second. Together they swept the inky darkness ahead. Directly ahead of us was a wall of barges. We were on the proverbial crash course. John climbed up onto the covers to get as good a view as I had. "Oh hell he's going to T-bone the fleet!"

"Oh shit, I forgot to steer!" came out of the night air through the loudspeaker.

Not wanting to get hit with snapping wires I stopped short of the coupling and turned back to see the collision.

John caught up to me said "How can he say he forgot to steer? The damn tow is swinging like a top."

"Yup and he's headed straight for the fleet at full speed!"

Both *Katie's* main engines were straining against the headway in full reverse, but the wheels were sucking air and we didn't slow down. There was a loud bang and the sickening groan of steel scraping steel with the force of many thousands of tons. I fell forward onto my knees as the initial impact turned into a gentle surge. In the darkness we heard the rifle-like retort of steel cables snapping. It takes a lot of force to break cables as thick as a man's wrist.

When everything got quiet, we were stuck on top of the other barge. The sloped rake of our barge had scraped barely up and over the side of the fleeted barge, slowing us to a stop without doing any serious damage at the point of contact.

"Aww shit!" John was holding on tight to the side of a cover.

"We're going to be chasing barges all the way to Hastings," I said.

"Let's go see the damage," John answered.

It took less than five minutes to walk around our lead barge and look in all the tanks for water. We got lucky, all the dents and cracks were above the waterline. This one wouldn't sink at least.

"Okay Johnny let's go check the fleet."

The *Itasca* working the fleets in South St. Paul.

We signaled the pilot to back off of the tow and steer up alongside these barges to tie off. After some more squeals from the abused steel hulls, we were separate once again and soon tied off. We were lucky not to be scrambling around in the dark chasing and pumping barges. There were broken wires and ratchets all over the place, but most of the rigging held, and the barges stayed together.

Once our two barges were tied off, we spent over an hour walking the fleet checking for damage and lifting up wing-tank hatch covers looking for sinkers, but found none.

All that was left to do was split up and check tanks and shore wires on the bank-side barges.

John took the alley between two stings of barges to check tanks, and I walked the outside next to the bank. I stepped over a kevel with a muddy shore wire wrapped around in a series of figure eights. A few feet past it was a hatch cover. As I was twisting and lifting the manhole cover with both hands, I held my flashlight in my mouth.

While bent over I heard a low growl. My hands were full, so I lifted my head to shine the light ahead of me. In the beam appeared two red glowing eyes. The hatch dropped from my hands when I fell backwards. The light bounced on the deck and rolled into the river. In the dark I saw the shadow disappear.

John hurried around the corner. "What's wrong?"

"I dunno something growled at me."

He swung his light around and caught the outline of a raccoon crawling back ashore paw over paw along the tight shore wire. "That's it. I've had enough scares for one night. Let's get back on the boat!"

"Do you really think we're any safer there with T-Bone the Zombie at the controls?"

"Zombies, monsters or ghosts, I don't care. I just want to get home and get some sleep."

The next time John and I saw Willy, he started right in on us. "What the hell did you clowns do out there to that fleet?"

"You're kidding right?" John's mouth dropped to his chest.

"Did you ask your pilot? What the hell are you asking us for? Put an exhausted crew out on a boat at night and you got the nerve to piss and moan when something goes wrong."

Willy sneered back at me. "Oh, is that all you can do is to whine and make excuses?"

John and I stiffened and looked sideways at each other. Later I said to him, "I wanted to strangle that little bastard!"

He snickered back, "Good thing you didn't, because I would have committed a cardinal sin — I would have enjoyed it."

"Well, Willy has always been a little jealous of towboaters from back in the day when he drove the hot-dog boats and Big Red threw him out of the pilothouse."

As we walked through the parking lot side-by-side John threw his arm across my chest, stopping me. "You gotta tell me that story."

"Oh it's a good one, trust me. Do you know Red?"

"I worked with Red back at the Harbor Circus, but I never heard that story."

Big Red, aka
Captain Buzz Low

The biggest character in the St. Paul harbor during the 1970s was Big Red. He was a big man, and his round ruddy face was surrounded by a full flaming-red beard. From the center of that beard jutted a well chewed cigar that twirled and bounced when he spoke. When standing at the pilothouse console between the sticks of his towboat, he would bark short gung-ho statements like "Full ahead!" and "Drive her Cappy!" while the cigar bobbed up and down. He is a legend among local river rats and was the subject of many river tales.

The first Big Red story I ever heard was about the time he drove his motorcycle on a wild ride through St. Paul. A bunch of the river rats had been partying hard at the old River Serpent.

The River Serpent was a blues-n-booze joint on Raspberry Island just a few feet from the swirling waters of the Mississippi. It was the top floor of the old Rowing Club. The building was built back in the 1870s. The island itself is right under the Wabasha Street Bridge, and the old red-tiled roof is still the most noticeable thing about it.

Red's partner in crime that night was another legend named Larry Hatrack. After storming out of the River Serpent one night, Red and Larry crawled aboard Red's motorcycle. Red adjusted his World War I aviator cap and pulled the goggles down over his eyes.

"You ready Hatrack?"

"Put the hammers down Red!"

Red wound his way off the island and across Wabasha to Kellogg Street, where he took a right turn and headed down towards Robert Street Bridge.

"Whaddaya doing Red? We gotta go the other way."

Big Red

Red turned onto the bridge and stopped. Hatrack had no idea what he was planning. While Hatrack tried to talk him out of it, Red wrestled the front wheel of his Suzuki 750 Water Buffalo up and over the curb onto the sidewalk. The front wheel rested against the foot of the arch where it grew out of the bridge deck.

Robert Street Bridge was built in 1925, or so the carvings at the top of the stone pillars read. It connects downtown St. Paul with the river bottoms of the West Bank.

The bridge site divides the steamboat landing levee into two: The Lower Landing was where the northbound steamers from St. Louis dropped passengers and cargo. The Upper Landing was where the smaller steamboats that serviced Minneapolis and towns along the Minnesota River arrived and departed.

The bridge flies and bounces across the gorge in a series of wide arches. Like a bouncing ball, the first arch is taller and wider than the last three. The tallest arch over the channel rises through the roadway and above the road. It's about six feet wide and 20 feet high.

Red had guided tows of barges under the bridge hundreds of times and he had driven across it thousands, but that night he had a desire to fly over the bridge.

"That thing is wide enough to drive over, Larry."

"You don't have the balls Red!"

Red growled over his shoulder, "I don't huh?"

Red gunned the throttle and proceeded to wrestle his Suzuki 750 up and over one of the Robert Street Bridge arches with Larry perched over the back wheel. Bystanders were reported to have heard Larry screaming at him the whole way.

Arch of the Robert Street Bridge.

I was there the night Big Red and a gang of us took over the *Jonathan Padelford* in midstream and kicked Captain Willy out of his pilothouse. It was the first appearance I witnessed of his alter ego: Captain Buzz Low.

Another local river rat had gotten hitched, and they threw the reception on board the Padelford. It started out as a civil enough affair. A small combo played some Dixieland jazz. Guests began discarding tuxedo coats and high heeled shoes as the booze flowed and the night wore on.

One of the few singles aboard, I headed up to the second deck to enjoy being out of doors on the river and not working. The J.P. is a genuine sternwheeler, and I was enjoying the slow rhythm of the big red paddlewheel and the rainbows thrown into the hot summer air as the buckets whooshed by slowly.

At some point Captain Willy decided to launch into the typical river narration performed for the tourists on the day trips. Groans traveled up the staircase from the salon of the first deck. It contained riveting stories about this bridge and that landing and such information that we were all well acquainted with and, in some instances, knew the real stories or knew the towboating version.

Behind me I heard a scuffling sound and heavy footsteps on the stairwell.

"Come on kid we're going upstairs to see the pilothouse!" said Big Red as he and a few other towboaters rushed up the narrow stairs to the upper deck. I looked to see him standing at the stairs swaying slightly with a plastic beer cup in one hand and motioning to me with the other. He was wearing his World War I leather flying hat and goggles. Immediately I sensed fun and shenanigans. Turned out I was right.

Once inside the pilothouse the phalanx of towboaters nonchalantly shouldered Willy away from the console and out the other side door. Red quickly closed the door and locked it. Willy's face drooped when he realized what was happening. Red waved playfully at Willy and then leaned forward into the public address microphone.

"Folks this is Captain Buzz Low, and I want to welcome you all to an evening of fun with the Low Brothers Flying Circus."

A huge roar of approval surrounded the boat. For a half hour he told about the sites along the historic riverfront from his unique perspective, while Willy begged outside the door. Instead of passing along history about Fort Snelling and Zebulon Pike, Red told tales about the time the *Harry R. Harris* burned and an engine room explosion threw Senator into the river, and about the hooker who plied her trade from a convenient houseboat below Omaha Bridge, and where so and so was when he fell in the river and got run over by a barge.

The whole time Buzz was regaling the wedding guests with his insider knowledge, Willy sulked outside the pilothouse. Finally Buzz scowled, "Aw let him in boys, before he starts crying again."

At last the boys felt bad and let Willy back in. The invitations for towboat pilots to view the pilothouse dwindled after that.

Circus Acts

When I first met Big Red he was port captain for a company called Minnesota Harbor Service. All the river rats called it "The Circus." He was bigger than life and twice as loud. He hired me to be a deckhand because he knew my dad.

There were two things everyone knew about Big Red: First, he was a wild man, and second, he loved to fly. Since his Vietnam days Red was enthralled with flying. He told me how he used to watch the chopper pilots come and go, just itching to be in that seat.

Piloting on the river was just never enough excitement for Red. He dreamed of flying all the time. One of our favorite drinking activities was to sit around a big table and plan his next excursion: The Low Brothers Flying Circus. He wanted to resurrect the days of barnstorming. We had all seen the movie about those days, "The Great Waldo Pepper." The more empty pitchers of beer that appeared on the table, the more outrageous became the stunts we designed.

The accuracy of memories has dimmed over time, but it seems to me the last idea for the Circus involved wing walking strippers donning parachutes and landing in the waiting crowd.

It wasn't always just talk though. He once got me into the backseat of his Champion Citabria, and we went buzzing around the St. Croix River Valley.

Red pulled off a few good snap rolls, and then we saw something ahead that grabbed his attention. A few miles ahead a highway bridge stretched across the valley. It seemed to leap across the deep gorge. The bridge was an arch with a lot of space between the bridge deck and the St. Croix River.

Red put the bird into a steep dive yelling back at me, "Whaddya think Bobby, can we make her?"

I answered not as I was inclined to, but as I thought he'd appreciate. Instead of screaming, "Are you fucking crazy!" I said in my best imitation of a snarl, "Go ahead. We gotta die some day."

Throughout the maneuver I thought I could hear Red going "Ra-tatatatatatatat." The only other time I'd experienced a tighter turn was when my Dad took me up for some loops in his own Citabria.

Some of his wild character came out in elaborate practical jokes. One of his more creative pranks took a disturbing turn in front of a small crowd in the early morning before crew change. About a dozen of us had shown up early to drink the free crummy coffee before we drove all over the river valley trying to find boats.

The yelling and screaming started above us. Soon it escalated and we heard doors slamming and footsteps hurrying down the metal stairs. Then we saw Jack Hickey, the company's marine draftsman and a flying buddy of Big Red's, come around the corner from the stairway. He ran to a spot just outside of the crew room and turned to hurl one final insult at Red, who was rounding the corner behind him.

Standing where we could see him clearly through the door, a horrified look came to his face. "Red, Red, what are you doing Red? Please Red, don't!"

"I've had it with you Jack. You've messed with me for the last time!" With that he stepped into view brandishing a pistol, which he promptly fired twice, "BANG - BANG," at the draftsman. Jack stumbled back a few steps and fell out of our sight. Red stepped forward and fired again.

Several paper cups of piping hot coffee hit the floor at the same time. What the others thought I don't know, but I wondered who'd get it next. Red stood there in front of the open door breathing heavily, his face beet red.

After a couple of seconds of dead silence, we quietly approached Red. His breathing seemed to slow. Each of us stood up and crept towards the door. Someone whispered "My God Red, what have you done?"

He turned to us until the pistol was pointed into the crowd. As one we stepped back. "What do you mean?" he growled. At which point he turned and stalked over to the body. With his boot he prodded roughly at the cadaver. "Get up Jack, I think we scared 'em alright."

Jack rolled over, got to his knees then stood to wipe off his pants. Then he did a sort of a "Tah dah!" pose and a bow. We all groaned and slunk back into the crew room.

That was my first short work period at the Circus. I was only there a few weeks between Twin City Barge going out of business and working for Capitol Barge. I didn't get to see much of Red that first year at CBS.

Big Red and his Capitol Idea

Sometime during my second season as Crash's full-time whipping boy I got a huge break when Big Red came over to Capitol to pilot the other shift on the *Harry R. Harris*. Someone in the office took pity on me and switched me over to Red's watch. Paddlefoot piloted the other boat, the *Mike Harris*, during the same shift as us.

Paddlefoot and Red loved to work the same shift. The radio between the *Mike Harris* and the *Harry R. Harris* was abuzz with plans for after work. After a night shift the routine was to gather at Dodi's on the West Side and hash over the night watch. The morning after the big wind storm we had a lot to discuss.

Red had come out of the Minnesota River shoving two loads with the *Harry R. Harris*. Senator and I were his deck crew. Paddlefoot was on the *Mike Harris* a couple miles behind us with three loads. Both tows were bound for American Commercial Barge Line's airport fleet, across the river from the Mounds Park overlook.

ACBL's fleet was several thousand feet of shoreline skirting the ends of the corporate-jet runways at the St. Paul Airport. Each shore wire was anchored to a sturdy piling. The pilings were set two hundred feet apart, and in the middle of each long wire was a floating steel barrel.

When Red got his tow of two loads abreast of the uppermost barrels, he began backing up full astern to stop. Senator and I came out of the galley with our grab hook to start fishing for the ends of the shore wires. When I tried to step up onto the barge from the bow of the *Harry*

R. Harris, a gale-force wind knocked me backwards. About the time the barges slowed down, this minor hurricane blowing straight off of the runways began to blow the loaded barges across the river to the old Farmers Union Two Dock.

"Come on Junior, let's see if we can get upstairs and see what Red's gonna do now."

Pigs Eye Bridge

We fought our way down the side of the small towboat and pulled ourselves up the stairs. We went into the leeward side of the pilothouse to save the windward door from being torn out of our hands. Even with all the doors and windows closed tightly, the sound of the wind was nearly deafening.

By then the loads were sailing sideways towards the long curved cement seawall below Dayton's Bluff. Red chewed and rotated the stub of his cigar between his teeth. "Well boys, she just might snap in two here when we hit the wall."

The ends of the tow landed hard on the wall. The barges rocked one way and then the other. The wires at the coupling twisted and groaned over the sound of the wind as the two barges tried to land flush on the curved wall. Red pulled the three main engines back to neutral. By some miracle the fore and aft wires held the barges together.

With the tow at a standstill, Red used the engines to twist the stern off of the wall and out to the middle of the river. It was a Herculean struggle for the *Harry R. Harris*, but after many long minutes the tow was backed into the wind. Then Red used all engines full astern to back straight across the river into the wind. Senator and I set up on the barge with our hook ready to get a wire. We had to lean almost horizontally to stay in one spot.

It took almost an hour for Red to jockey the face of the tow into the wind and back across the river 600 feet.

Senator and I got a shore wire onto the upstream end and wrapped it up on the stern. Red eased off the engines and immediately the wind blew the tow tight into the wire. The wind was still strong enough to push the downstream end up against the current until the loads, sitting nine feet in the forceful current, were crossways in the river.

It took nearly another half hour just to push the two loads flat against the wind and get some more shore wires wrapped up. By then Paddlefoot was almost down to the fleet with his three-piece unit.

Red got on the radio, "I better help you get landed, Paddlefoot. The wind is blowing too hard down here."

"She's windy, huh?"

"It blew my loads across the crick like they were empties. Yeah, it's windy down here."

Paddlefoot made his downstream approach and began to back in. Red positioned the *Weird Harry* against the head of his tow and started to push full ahead. With both boats working at full power the wind slapped the whole rig up against the seawall again. From there it took a half an hour just to work across the river and secure these loads to the first two. Finally the wind died down to a mere typhoon, and Red was at last able to help get Paddlefoot's tow flattened out and tied next to ours.

Red Scare

Sometimes when I would be sitting in the pilothouse behind Big Red, I would look under the red seat cushions and dig out the chart book. In every pilothouse is a copy of the Corps of Engineers' *Upper Mississippi River Navigation Charts*. These poster-sized flip books are full of crossings and landings, each with a unique name that refers to a character, an event or a local geographic feature. Without a background in the area, it is sometimes hard to know the reason for the name.

There are several such places in the Twin Cities that locals are unaware of and that younger river rats know by name, places like Monkey Rudder Bend at Hidden Falls.

Red had a place in the St. Paul harbor named in his honor. His place in river history is secure because of his greatest fear. A landing was named for this fear.

There is a spot near the mouth of the Minnesota River that has been a traditional place to change harbor towboat crews for as long as I can remember. It is only a few hundred feet downstream, or east, of the Mendota Bridge. For the crew coming aboard, it is accessible through a tunnel in the railroad levee next to the historic Sibley House. It is across the river from Pike Island and viewable from the parapets of Fort Snelling.

It is also a half hour from downtown St. Paul and two hours from the port of Savage, so for a towboat crew having put in 12 hours already, it can be a handy place to get off the boat. It has also been the scene of some historic towboat adventures while crews simply got on and off the boat.

Whether northbound with empties for Savage grain terminals or southbound with the loaded grain barges, a typical crew change has the pilot backing the tow to a stop. Then he allows the deckhands to "knock the boat out" and remove the face wires that hold the towboat securely to the barges.

In normal pool water, the barges sit relatively still while the boat shoves up against the cut bank and the two crews are able to swap spots. Easy come easy go.

During one of these crew changes the crew parked the pickup truck in front of the Sibley House and walked under the railroad overpass. On the other side of this short tunnel is the thick river-bottom forest, more of a jungle really, of the Minnesota River. Stopping to adjust his load or tie his shoes, Red fell behind the group.

At the boat, the night crew greeted the oncoming deckhands.

"Hey, good morning. Where's Captain Red?"

"Don't know. He was right behind us."

They continued their crew-change palaver, and no one thought any more about Red. After a time the pilot left the controls and came down to the crew room and asked about Red.

They all looked into the jungle of cottonwoods and elms, but no one could see Red.

Soon enough the woods were filled with a blood curdling scream. It was a scream those men still talk about to this day. It made them wonder if a small animal was being torn apart alive.

Suddenly Red flew from the top of the levee and landed on the head deck with a powerful thud. In his eyes was the look of a man who has seen the devil himself. He sprang to his feet, raced up the stairs to the pilothouse and slammed the doors. He locked himself in, and it was hours before he would allow anyone to enter.

When at last the deck crew could see him, he was still pale and bathed in a cold sweat. It seems that as he was gulping for air and trying to clear his head. He had spooked a snake. "It was a damn rattler!" though years later he allowed as how it could have been a garter snake for all he knew. A mere glimpse of the tail disappearing into the grass had elicited his overwrought reaction.

His fear of snakes had developed during his tours in Vietnam, where he'd had some nightmare experiences in Viet Cong tunnels, where some very poisonous snakes were often used in traps.

Since then that place has been known to St. Paul river rats as the "Snake Farm."

Red Baiting

Red was determined that I would be a pilot, so on the few breaks from Crash, Red would have me steer the boat. When I apprenticed at Twin City Barge, I had already done a fair bit of steering for Lucky in Chicago and Skeeter over on the Tennessee River, but Red was posting me in the harbor. His lessons were as good as any I got from Lucky and Skeeter and had the added benefit of being practical, since I planned to work in the St. Paul harbor.

These lessons bothered the hell out of Crash, who saw me as a threat for some demented reason only he could understand. Red's style was the exact opposite of how Crash stood between the sticks. Where Crash was nervous and would freeze with indecision, Red would turn loose, put the hammers down and trust his instincts to steer out of trouble. And it worked. It was only a matter of time before these two clashed — like matter and anti-matter.

Decking for Big Red was enjoyable. Gruff on the exterior, he had a cool and calm attitude about piloting that Crash simply didn't have in him. After a few weeks of decking, he began to encourage me to steer. He was showing me how to handle the boat in the fleets, which is the hardest thing to learn.

Crash sabotaged Red's and my efforts by complaining to Draine-O at every bend about how my time between the sticks was hurting the work on deck.

Steering does take away from time in the engine room, but that is a tradition on the river. You learn to pilot by steering and learning from an experienced pilot. Red and Harry did me a great favor by allowing me to practice at their expense. And they were incredibly patient with me in the process — something Crash never could be.

One hot afternoon Red and Harry spent a painful couple of hours picking up shore wires in Packing-House and North Star fleets in South St. Paul. Red wanted me to experience the challenge of digging barges out of a crowded fleet. One barge in particular had been a real beast to get at. It was lodged in between a couple of tiers at an odd angle, which caused no end of banging around. All the while Red handled lines and assisted Harry as he directed me from the deck.

The two of them came around the corner after getting totally whipped by a shore wire as kinky as a Hollywood marriage. This was not easy for Red, as he was much heavier than during his days as a warrior in Vietnam.

Neither spoke for a minute as they caught their breaths.

"Okay kid, look on the clipboard and find that next barge."

I looked over the orders and began to look to the sides and behind the boat at the surrounding empty barges.

"What's the number?"

"RW-238," I read from the list.

"See it anywhere?" he asked.

"Nooope. I looked up at the two of them standing on the end of a barge across from the open pilothouse window. Harry slowly grew a large grin and tugged on Red's sleeve. As Red turned towards him, Harry sidestepped a yard or two and pointed at a set of large white numbers painted on a primer-red bulkhead. It read RW-238. I will never forget that number. Certain barge numbers stick in a river rat's mind. CC-7812 is the first barge I took a corner out of years later, and RW-238 is the barge Red didn't strangle me over.

They each cussed me in frustration and then walked back down the bank side to unwrap the steel cables they had just sweated blood over.

Steering didn't bother me, because he was right behind me in case I made a mistake. But because Crash was trying to squash my steering, he began to work on me to quit Capitol and seek a pilot's job somewhere else in the harbor. "Hell Junior, if that dope Crash can handle a boat, you sure as hell can!"

It all came to a head one evening as the temperature was dropping. Tempers rose between Red and Crash, because Crash did not want me getting a leg up into the pilothouse.

Red motioned me to nose the *Harry R. Harris* into the sea wall below Mounds Park Bluff. "We're crew changing right here at Farmer's two-house," he radioed over channel 18 to the Capitol Barge houseboat.

I went down to check the oil levels in the engines and gearboxes, while Harry Baxter climbed upstairs to paint some fresh red paint on the starboard side of the pilothouse wing.

Finished with the engines, I went upstairs to the pilothouse to wait for the night crew. Red was unscrewing the little round knobs that sit atop the Westinghouse air controls for the main engines. He leaned back in his chair and started to juggle the three little black caps he had unscrewed. Wearing a big grin he just sat there juggling and whistling.

I could tell that Crash was bugged when the truck pulled up at the dock. When he saw me in the pilothouse, he hightailed down the ladder onto the head deck and scurried up to the pilothouse. Red motioned me to follow him, and as Crash came in one door we ducked out the other door. Red hustled us up the ladder, and we were off the boat in record time.

"I don't feel like talking to that boob tonight. The orders are simple, enough even he can't possibly screw them up."

The three of us stood on the wall and traded pleasantries with Senator and the other night deckhand. Crash jumped out onto the bridge wing and yelled, "Hey Red, what am I supposed to do with these?" He was holding the three throttle caps like they were an artifact from antiquity and held the answer to some fantastic riddle.

Red with a huge grin on his face pointed back at Crash, "Ya know you're standing on wet paint, don't you?"

Crash looked down at his cowboy boots and then at his footprints leading from the door. He began to hop from one foot to another completely dumbfounded as to where to go. Up on the wall, we were laughing loud enough to attract the deckhands from the galley. They came out onto the head deck and looked up to see Crash dancing like some kind of demented gorilla.

Senator looked up at Crash, who was still hopping rapidly from one foot to the other. "Hey Crash, not bad. Now you just need to work on the juggling part, and you're ready for vaudeville."

Crash grew redder than Red's beard. "I'll get you for this. You'll pay for this!"

Red slowly shook his head as he turned to get into the truck. "Ahhh that stupid sunnovabich has got a bad case of the Red-Ass!"

Between the Sticks in Minneapolis

At the houseboat the next morning, in front of everyone, Crash made a huge scene about me steering for Big Red. Draine-O did not appear eager to get involved, but he had to do or say something. He questioned Red about whether my steering interfered with my engine room chores. Red said the boat ran fine for him, and he would teach whomever he wanted to steer the river. Crash got hysterical. Draine-O declared a moratorium on steering.

That settled it for Red. He quit on the spot. "No one tells me how to run a boat. I am out of here. Crash, if you got a hair on your ass, you'll follow me up the ramp and we'll settle this the old fashioned way in the parking lot."

Crash sort of slid quietly behind Draine-O, and Red stomped off up the ramp.

Crash glared at me and spat, "You're steering days are over!"

Draine-O frowned and went back into his office. "You all clear out I have to go run a boat now."

Crash brushed by me on his way out the door and flashed me a malicious grin.

After that I had little to no chance to get into the wheelhouse of a Capitol boat. The next pilothouse openings Draine-O had went to a couple of older guys. They deserved their shot as much as I did, but I saw the writing on the wall. The only way Draine-O would ever let me run one of his boats was if I could prove myself somehow, and that would have to be somewhere else.

There were piloting jobs to be had in the harbor, because of the barge boom of the 1970s. But at the age of 21, I was viewed as a risk by boat and barge owners.

Well Big Red had me convinced I was ready, or at least ready to pretend I was ready, for command. How many times had I heard him exclaim, "If that idiot Crash can run a boat you sure as hell can!"?

He called me the summer after after the blow-up in the office to tell me about an open shift on a boat running from St. Paul to Minneapolis through the locks every day. It would be good experience and twice the wages of a deckhand. That was tempting, since my mother was divorced and struggling to make ends meet. When I hesitated he said, "Think about how much you can help your mom with the extra money."

I had to at least try.

I was nervous when I walked down the ramp to the houseboat at the High Bridge on that day in July 1980 to confront Draine-O about letting me have more responsibility. It was boom times on the river, and I wanted a piloting job running a towboat and two barges through the locks in Minneapolis. That spring he allowed me to run the little *Arlene* at a dock way back in Pigs Eye Lake. It was off the main channel of the river. Switching empties and loads from the same dock all day long was all I did. Once in a great, great while, when we got a break and limped to the end of the slip for diesel fuel, I would just get a glimpse of the Mississippi and the big towboats heading up or downstream. Chained to the one dock with baby *Arlene* seemed like small-time piloting, and I was hungry for something more exciting.

I was headed down to tell Draine-O, my boss, that I was quitting to take a job on the *Paul Lambert*. The *Tall Paul* was three times as long as the *Arlene* and had twice the horsepower. It was a big boat and mastering the boat and the locks would be a huge challenge for a 21-year-old kid.

He was standing outside on the wharf barge tied next to the houseboat. Out in the river the *Mike Harris* had gone past the houseboat and was going under the Smith Avenue High Bridge. Admiring his red-and-white boats while listening to the sounds of the engines he fussed over like a mother hen brought him a simple joy.

I knew his history well, because he loved to tell stories and his office was a small museum dedicated to his life as a sailor. After a stint in the Navy, he became a licensed engineer on the old *Hugh C. Blaske*, running up and down the Upper Miss for years. His office on the red-and-white houseboat was filled with brass mementos, and towboat pictures and paintings. My brother had done one large painting of the towboat he named after his mother, the *Lois E.* It showed her (the boat) going upriver without barges. Next to it he kept a framed photograph of a young Draine-O on the head deck of the old *Hugh C.* He was bare-chested astride his pride and joy motorcycle, an Aerial Square Four. He had talked the captain into letting him bring it aboard for a trip. He and his mates had lashed it down between the capstan and the door to the forward deck locker room.

Always frugal and a hard worker, he was eventually able to acquire his own small fleet of harbor towboats. He hung them outside of a houseboat and ratty old barge he used for a wharf and shop. He anchored down under the Smith Avenue High Bridge and operated there for over 15 years.

I felt strongly that because I had lasted two of those years working for Crash, that madman pilot of his, that I deserved a shot at running one of his other boats.

"Bob," I blurted because I had to get it out or it would get stuck in my throat aground on my fear, "I want a pilot job. There is an opening on the *Paul Lambert*, and I am going to ask for it."

He stood between me and the river and folded his thick arms across his barrel chest. "Don't quit now. Be patient, you'll get your turn."

"Well, I heard that Timberhead Ed is looking for someone to pilot the *Paul Lambert* on the Minneapolis run. If all you can tell me is to be patient, then I'm going to ask for that job." I was secretly hoping he would put me on one of his bigger boats.

He called my bluff. "Go ahead. There's the phone. Give him a call."

He followed me into the houseboat, and with shaky fingers I swallowed hard and dialed the guy up. "Time to put up or shut up, Deckster," I thought to myself.

"Well Bob, have you run the locks up there?" Timberhead asked me.

"No, I haven't." I was feeling very uncomfortable as Draine-O stood just a few feet away glaring at me.

I looked back at him and suddenly I was pissed off enough to say whatever it took to get out of that shit-hole lake and onto a boat that did some real towboating,

"Well do you think you can handle it?" he came back.

"Sure I can."

The head deck of the *Lois E* (with Joe).

The next morning I was staring into the belly of the beast that is the curved long wall of the upper lock at St. Anthony Falls. Off to my left the water slipped swiftly and turbulently over the dam. My knees were turning to jelly. The lock men had swung open the big round sign on the upstream end of the lock wall. It signaled a nasty little out draft of current that pulls the barges towards the dam. I could see the greasy, slippery current sweep pieces of drift away from the wall and out towards the dam.

Four hundred feet ahead of me, Jeff was giving me hand signals and getting ready to try and stop me with a thick lock line if anything went wrong. There was no way out for me. I had to stay where I was and concentrate on his hands. At the same time, I had to look all around to make sure the cross current of the dam didn't get a hold of the tow and jerk us the wrong way. The slightest miscalculation and poor Jeff the deckhand would take the brunt of the punishment when 3,000 tons of steel smashed into many more tons of cement. He'd have been wadded up into a steel ball as easily as you can crumple a sheet of paper.

This must be what old Captain Skeeter was warning me about — the ghosts — this haunting fear of responsibility. All the old timers I steered for would tell me, "Anyone can steer a boat up and down the river. Hell my mama can stand there and steer. And better'n you judging from the shape of your wake. Fer gawds sake boy, a snake would get cramps trying to follow you upstream! Wait until you're on your own — until there's no one settin' behind ya to save yer ass from yourself. Then you're a river pilot!"

Well this is it. This is what I asked for. I am standing atop the twin 600-horsepower diesel mains of the *Tall Paul Lambert*. The engines are quietly chuffing away, oblivious of what they are a party to, driving us ever closer to disaster. In a few moments I am going to stuff acres worth of steel between two narrow lock walls.

Only a half hour earlier we had slipped loose our mooring lines in the small fleet of the Port of Minneapolis. We steered through Lowry, the Soo Line Railroad, Broadway and Plymouth Avenue bridges, all pretty straight shots. But the last few bridges above the lock will test a pilot's mettle.

The navigation span of the Great Northern Railroad Bridge is up against Nicollet Island. But then the pilot needs to steer all the way over to the downtown side and pass under Hennepin by the post office.

On his way out to ride the head into the lock, the deckhand, Jeff, gave me a casual all clear signal as he walked past the Great Northern Bridge fence. I lowered the retractable pilothouse to duck the low railroad span and raised it back in time to see De LaSalle High School on our left. Nicollet Island at that time was under the influence of a gentrification movement. The old places were being renovated and new condos had been built along the river. Beneath the steep bank under these upscale attempts, a couple of homeless men were engaged in a long tradition of sleeping one off on the grass of the river bank.

Under the big Grain Belt Beer sign, high school students between classes lounged about smoking cigarettes. This was my audience. They waved and pulled at window shades in the air coaxing me to blow the horn for them. I waved and thought, "They sure have it easy." To them I probably seemed to be living the easy life, gliding down the river.

I cranked the rudders hard over and started the big tricky right-hand steer to fight the current and get to the other side of the river. Wheel wash from the twin, 64-inch propellers rolled up onto the rocky bank of the island. We slid on over to the right bank and glided past the post office promenade. This was where even more hobos lounged on park benches and drank cheap wine. When they were drunk and the bottles were dry, they stumbled down to sleep in the little caves scoured out under the road by high water.

I felt a little surge of courage from having gotten past the spot that ruined Crash not too many years before. Before long I could see down into the elbow of the long wall. From Hennepin you cannot see past the curve into the chamber. Standing up with both hands sweating all over the steering levers my knees began to wobble slightly more.

"There is no way that it will fit in there" I am thinking over and over to myself, because no one is sitting behind me to tell me if I am in good shape or not. This is my mess. I looked out over the empty lazy bench at the stern to sense any lateral motion. "Are we sliding too fast into the wall?" I asked the empty bench where Skeeter and Red used to sit and advise me. I wondered momentarily if these were the same fears faced by every rookie pilot. So I took a deep breath and just pointed at the bend in the wall.

Jeff calmly continued to raise his arms up high and signal my distance from the wall. An instant before the tow made contact with the wall, Jeff on the bow and John on the stern dropped their rope fenders in at the same time and the tow landed evenly. There was surprisingly little noise to indicate that 6,000 tons had just landed on the long wall. All I felt in the pilothouse was a slight sideways surge. Then the bumpers rolled out from between the barges and the wall. That's when the high pitched squeal and accompanying pops and wrenching sounds started as all that steel began rub the bare cement. As the dust rolled up into the air, I could smell the burning cement and yellow government paint.

When Jeff signaled clear of the bullnose, I dropped the throttles into full reverse. The guys wrapped their lines up between the barges and the floating timberheads. I dropped into the pilot's chair and a pool of sweat.

Well, I had that first one under my belt. The rest would be easier. I couldn't resist a snotty little smile at how my success would dig at Crash. Most guys don't get the wheelhouse until their 30s or even 40s, and here I was, in July 1980, sitting between the sticks in command of a powerful diesel towboat at 22. Despite his efforts to deny me a shot at the wheelhouse, I was now the youngest pilot in the harbor.

Jeff looked up at me from the head deck after he had tied the boat to the side of the lock. Behind us the great steel chamber doors slowly swung shut.

"Not bad for a green rookie pilot!" he grinned at me.

Growing up on Air Force bases all over the country, except in the Midwest, I never expected to be driving big boats for a living, but here I was. I remembered all the old timers who used to tell me I'd never make it, that "ya can't make a pilot outta no damn book." And they were right. It was working with men like Red who made a pilot out of me. Even Crash taught me how not to be a pilot and to lead by example, not by screaming.

"Hey, I didn't hit anything! I'm already ahead of Crash's learning curve."

The St. Louis Shuffle

A couple months later, after knocking around the locks and trying to sleep in the cramped little bunkrooms of the *Tall Paul*, I was ready for the winter layoff. Then I got a phone call from Big Red.

"Get your ass down here boy. I need a second mate."

"Who is this?"

"It's Red, and I'm down here in St. Louis faced up to 15 empties, but I need some deckhands. Have Shwabby send you down here."

It didn't take much coaxing to get me out of the approaching cold weather and headed south. There are a lot of red-and-white DC-9s that shuttle between the Saints.

When I arrived at one of the riverside wharves in St. Louis, the crew was finishing up rigging 15 empty barges to shove up to St. Paul.

The *Nebraska City* was 125 feet long and carried about 4,200 horsepower. She had but one main deck, and the pilothouse sat by itself on stilts 30 feet in the air. I learned later that it had been an Illinois River boat originally, and the pilothouse was on a hydraulic ram that raised and lowered it for all the low bridges on that river. A few years earlier a pilot had not lowered it enough and tore it loose. When the owners had it repaired, they just welded it in the raised position. So, the boat had one of those ungainly profiles where the pilothouse, from a distance, appears to be floating over the boat.

As the boat got closer to the wharf, I could see that Red was up in the pilothouse with the pilot named Woody.

"Welcome aboard Bobby! We're going across the river to face up and get northbound. Throw your stuff in the second bunkroom on the starboard side. Get some gloves, and we'll be facing up right away."

Woody leaned forward and grinned at me. I waved back. I knew him from when he had been a pilot at Twin City Barge. That company going out of business had scattered good crew all over the river.

So I stashed my bags in a bunkroom on the lower deck and made my way back to the galley to look around the boat. I did stop and watch from the galley door while we boated across that section of the river that inspired T.S. Eliot to proclaim the Mississippi a "strong brown god."

I took a deep breath of that fresh musty air that soon turned acrid as we neared the Illinois bank, where the refineries and chemical plants line the river bank from here to Grafton. The big line boat didn't roll as much as the smaller harbor tugs I was used to working. It felt pretty darn solid under my feet.

Red pointed the boat for a fleet across the river from the Arch. I helped face up the boat on the downstream end.

The mate then explained that I would be standing on Woody's watch, but that I should eat with Red's crew getting ready to come on watch. He needed to be on watch with Red, but he had been up all day. So I would work a few hours on Red's watch while he got a quick nap.

"Hell, by the time we get through lock 27, we'll all get a few days rest waiting on 26."

"Is it choked up?"

"It's the bottleneck of the universe," he joked, "boats lined up all the way down into the Chain of Rocks right now."

He went back to his bunkroom, after pointing out the running gear he wanted on the head of the empties. It took about 40 minutes to carry the running light set, lock lines, jack staff and depth sounders up the towknees and across the bow of the tow.

An hour later Woody was on watch, and we threw off the last of the shore wires. He let the current that shoves through the St. Louis harbor year round set the tow off the bank as he guided the barges upstream. Not more than a few minutes after we turned loose, the engineer came running out of the engine room yelling that one of the main engine gear boxes was rattling like an "old whore with bad dentures!"

We tied our tow of 15 empties off to a fleet across the river from the St. Louis Arch and headed up to the shipyard at Grafton, Illinois. Before we could go, I had to crawl down into the heat of the engine room with the engineer. He told me that we had to chain the shaft in place, so the propeller wouldn't free-wheel spin and grind up the bull gear more.

I squatted on the steel deck on one side of the refrigerator-sized gear-box and the fist-sized bolts where it was fastened to the main engine, as big as a truck. He handed me one end of the chain come-a-long, and I wrapped it around the 12-inch drive shaft that ran though the hull to the six-foot-wide propeller. It had been a couple years since I had stumbled around a line boat engine room. Everything was twice the size of the same stuff on a harbor boat.

"Wow. This is going to be a bear to work on," I remember thinking.

No sooner had we tied off at the shipyard than the engineers were down there tearing covers off of the gearbox to find handfuls of metal shavings and chunks of rubber from the gear teeth in the bottom of the pan.

All day long for a full week I sweated out the heat of the engine room. My job was to assist the engineer and the mechanics in hoisting the refrigerator sized gearbox clear of the starboard GM engine. The engine was the size of a pickup truck. I would fetch the arm-sized wrenches and ratchets while the pros did the thinking and tinkering. Sort of like a nurse, I was handing wrenches and cleaning parts to help the engineers tear apart and rebuild the bull gear.

By night we drank cheap beer in a cheap waterfront dive. Listening to river rats from different regions swap stories and compare notes is entertaining.

One afternoon the gearbox was given a clean bill of health and the engineer started the mains back up with the high squealed scream of the air starters. Red departed the shipyard and headed downstream light boat for the St. Louis harbor.

Across from the Arch we faced up to 15 empties and throttled up through the Eads Bridge and into the Chain of Rocks Canal. At Lock 27, Red slipped into the 1,200-foot-long chamber. As soon as the lines were secure the tow had risen a whole foot, and we were northbound again. Red had barely time to neutral.

"Wow!" I thought, "if the rest of the trip goes this smooth, we'll be in St. Paul again in no time at all."

Then we went past the asphalt docks of Wood River, Illinois, and stopped to wait on Lock 26, the "bottleneck of the world."

Sometime during this short transit Woody, the pilot, came down with a nasty flu-cold combo. It had him bedridden. I stood his watch, waiting in line to lock up through the small chambers of Lock 26. My job consisted of sitting in the pilothouse looking across the tow to a clump of trees on the bank to make sure the bow stayed planted on the muddy beach.

Every few hours I had to steer the stern in to lay flat along the bank, so a south-bound tow coming out of the lock had room to pass by us. Six hours on and six off for a couple of long days. Once in awhile, when I relieved Red, he would have leap-frogged up the bank a quarter mile or so.

It all seemed pretty easy. I sat there with my feet propped up on the console next to the throttles and listened to the marine radio for traffic. Mr. Big Shot, that was me. Even found one of Red's new cigars and took to chewing on it until I'd get nauseous. I found out that you don't even have to smoke them to get sick. Still, I thought, I looked cool and official with it clutched between my teeth while waving to a passing line boat. After four or five watches like this, I was beginning to think I could handle this job.

I knew nothing of guiding a raft of empties in a stiff breeze, to say nothing of handling loads southbound around a lock in a rising river with outdrafts or outwitting cross currents around bridge piers, but I figured I could learn all that stuff too.

I was sound asleep in my bunk dreaming about a couple of girls and towboats, when my door burst open and the room flooded with light from the hallway. Between blinks I could make out some imposing silhouettes in the doorway. Struggling to surface from my grogginess, I felt panic. The figures outlined in the light were big and menacing. Surely I was having a nightmare, but the physical tightening was too real.

Red's voice barked from the cluster, "Wake up Bobby. The Feds are arresting the vessel and say we gotta get off the boat!"

"Wh... what? We're under arrest?"

"No. The boat is under arrest."

"The boat is under arrest?"

Just as suddenly as they had appeared in my doorway, they were gone. I clawed my way out of bed. My head was reeling. What kind of a dream is this? I stood leaning against the door jamb rubbing my head when the mate appeared in front of me.

"What is going on?"

"You heard. We been arrested."

"We're going to jail?"

"No. They just want the boat."

"Why?"

"The boss hasn't paid the bills or the lease on the boat for a few months now, and the check, the big check for the repairs, bounced all the way from St. Louis to St. Paul, and now the Feds, these guys are taking custody of the vessel for the owners."

"Oh."

I stumbled back to galley and cupped a steaming mug of coffee between my hands. Standing in the open door in my underwear, I watched the river bank finally pass us by. Trouble was, we were going backwards.

It took a few hours for Red and the mate to back down near the mouth of the Missouri River and find some shore wires to secure the tow of 15 empty barges. Red docked the boat at National Marine's wharf in Wood River on the Illinois side.

The Feds watched as we packed and prepared to catch a van to the airport, and the boss finally showed up. He was in a tailored suit, and his wife was by his side. He was all grins and backslaps, but that didn't hold any sway over the G-men, and we were escorted off the impounded vessel at last.

In two weeks and a couple days we had covered over 60 miles on the

Upper Mississippi. Most of them were made without any barges in front of the boat. In the end, we netted 20 miles with no barge revenue, which blows the ton/mile advantage of river towing all to hell. To top it all off, the boss bounced all of our paychecks.

Later on his wife, with some family money behind her, signed us each a personal check. We owed it all to one poor slob who had to actually pitch a tent and camp out on the boss' front lawn. Only the embarrassment — when the neighbors saw him there in his wheelchair next to his camp stove — got him reimbursed for his medical expenses. He had broken both ankles when he jumped from an empty hull down to a loaded barge. The height proved too much, and the steel deck shattered both ankles.

Weeks later I bumped into my former deckhand Jeff Malm, and he told me how he finally got his bad checks made good. He had stalked the boss until he caught him coming home from a tennis date one afternoon. He followed him and his buddy into the house demanding his month's pay

"I'll mail you a check," Shwabby purred trying to keep from being embarrassed too much in front of his white-collar friend.

"Fuck you," Jeff retorted as he jacked the old boy up the wall by his Izod collared shirt. "I didn't mail you any fucking work!"

Fortunately for Shwabby, his wife happened on the scene about then, and with calm gained from recent experience cut Jeff one of her personal checks for his lost pay.

On the flight home from St. Louis, Red and I sat together on the plane. It was a DC-9 that banked hard taking off from St. Louis Airport. I looked down on the riverfront and saw the Gateway Arch as a line boat with 15 barges crawled past it.

"Well kid, that was a pretty weird trip, wasn't it?"

The incident was still puzzling to me. Just a few hours earlier I had been nestled in my bunk snoozing to the drone of the main engines, and now I was looking at a river full of ant-sized towboats while Pratt and Whitney jets whined in my ear.

"That dope actually told me to take all the rigging, lines, tools and pumps off the boat right there in front of the feds. I told him he was nuts."

"Hmmm," was all I could think to say.

"The only way I'm going to get a decent job and some livable wages is to start my own business. Ya know, Hatrack and Paddlefoot and me have been talking about getting some boats and doing our own hiring and run our own stuff. You interested?"

"I guess. I need a job next spring."

"Going to call it Pilot River. Whaddaya think? And now that Shwabby is out of business, I bet we can get a lease on the *Paul Lambert*."

The next season Big Red, Hatrack and Paddlefoot started their own company. They leased the harbor tugs *Itasca*, *Tall Paul Lambert* and *Katie Rose* from Twin City Barge. With these boats they ran the lower fleets and took over the work left in the Minneapolis Upper Harbor going back and forth between St. Paul and the new locks at St. Anthony Falls. They were heady new times in the Twin ports. There were many new opportunities and new problems of a business and political nature. The harbor got even more interesting over the next several years, with new characters and new adventures. I saw these happenings from between the sticks in the pilothouse, so the view was a little different.

I looked at Big Red with his ample belly and full red beard. Knowing his character, I thought of him as some sort of odd cross between Santa Claus and Wolf Larson. He was a gruff old river captain who sometimes took care of me like I was one of his own.

I looked out the window again. There were so many more wharf barges and stack logos nosing around the river around St. Louis. With all the new small companies in St. Paul, I knew I would find a job by spring. Whether it was working for Draine-O again or the Circus or the Toad and his dad at DBS, there were a dozen jobs to be had in the St. Paul harbor. And they would be a piloting jobs — jobs in a nice warm pilothouse between the sticks.

"What about you kid? What are you going to do?"

"I think I'm going to stay in St. Paul, Red. There's plenty of work up there. I can get a deckhand job easy enough this spring."

After all the flying I had done as a kid growing up while criss-crossing the country by jet, I was finally heading someplace that felt like home.

"Good. Because I am serious about starting my own company. But not on deck working for some chump like Crash. I'll have a pilot job for you. You need to be between the sticks."